"Having known and worked with Wayman Ming for several years, I can hear his pastoral and wise voice in this book. All of us are trying to discern God's voice through the noise of crazy politics, devastating pandemics and various forms of isolation. It is easy for fear, discouragement and hopelessness to be the dominant expressions. Thankfully, Wayman has given us a road map, based on God's eternal Word, with signposts from our contemporary culture. It's a map of hope, peace, truth and love. Enjoy the ride as you follow the map!"

Dr. Doug Beacham, general superintendent,
International Pentecostal Holiness Church

"While God's 'interruptions' in our lives often do not make sense to us, He desires that we seek Him in all circumstances: good, bad and ugly. *Nearer to God* challenges us to see these interruptions as invitations to a closer walk with God."

Pastor Samuel Rodriguez, lead pastor, New Season Worship
Center; president, National Hispanic Christian Leadership
Conference (NHCLC); author, *From Survive to Thrive*;
executive producer, *Breakthrough*

"I love Wayman Ming. I love his humility, his sincerity. He leads a global organization, yet his transparent, persistent hunger of more of God shines through. That's a New Testament leader. And it is the kind of author you want to read. His book is simple, straightforward, laced with stories, engaging. The further your reading takes you, the deeper the passionate call to a transforming relationship."

P. Douglas Small, president, Project Pray; international
coordinator, Church of God Prayer Ministries

T0311360

"My dear friend Wayman Ming has given us timely exhortations in his book *Nearer to God*, calling us to the vital place of finding God in these difficult times. He raises our expectancy for God encounters in the midst of challenges, and I know you will be blessed and strengthened!"

Bishop Robert Stearns, executive director, Eagles' Wings

"The magnetic power of God's love draws every human being. Jesus promised that He would "draw all men" to Him when He demonstrated His love by being lifted up on a cross. We all feel this supernatural pull toward God, yet many times we sense we are very far away from Him. In *Nearer to God*, Wayman Ming helps us close the gap and connect with God in fresh ways. From how God hears us from heaven to how we hear Him on earth, Ming challenges the reader to truly know God, not just talk about Him. Your life will be challenged by this book, and you will be blessed as you learn how to *draw near!*"

Dr. William M. Wilson; president, Oral Roberts University; chair, Pentecostal World Fellowship; global co-chair, Empowered21

"Creatively illustrating timeless themes with current application, my colleague and friend Wayman Ming calls us back to the profound simplicities of intimacy with the 'GodFather.' Every chapter of *Nearer to God* deals with a 'main thing' that I believe our Lord is calling the Church back to in these challenging yet opportune times. I pray we have ears to hear."

Rev. David R. Wells, M.A., D.D., general superintendent, Pentecostal Assemblies of Canada

Nearer to
GOD

Nearer to
GOD

CLOSING THE DISTANCE
BETWEEN YOU AND YOUR CREATOR

WAYMAN MING JR.

Chosen

a division of Baker Publishing Group
Minneapolis, Minnesota

© 2021 by Wayman Ming Jr.

Published by Chosen Books
11400 Hampshire Avenue South
Bloomington, Minnesota 55438
www.chosenbooks.com

Chosen Books is a division of
Baker Publishing Group, Grand Rapids, Michigan

Printed in the United States of America

Library of Congress Cataloging-in-Publication Data
Names: Ming, Wayman, Jr., author.
Title: Nearer to God : closing the distance between you and your Creator / Wayman Ming Jr.
Description: Minneapolis, Minnesota : Chosen, a division of Baker Publishing Group, [2021] | Includes bibliographical references.
Identifiers: LCCN 2020056634 | ISBN 9780800761851 (trade paperback) | ISBN 9781493433438 (ebook) | ISBN 9780800762483 (casebound)
Subjects: LCSH: God (Christianity)—Worship and love. | Faith. | Christian life.
Classification: LCC BV4817 .M56 2021 | DDC 248.4—dc23
LC record available at https://lccn.loc.gov/2020056634

21 22 23 24 25 26 27   7 6 5 4 3 2 1

For my wife, Kimberly,
who is a godly woman and my biggest encourager.

For my sons—Spencer and Garrett,
who are even now making an impact as godly men,
seeking to make a worldwide difference.

For my daughter, Grace,
who is God's special gift to her dad,
and a light in the midst of the darkness.

Contents

Foreword

All of us have friends or people we admire and desire to be closer with. They hold a special place in our hearts, and spending time with them is a treat, especially when it comes at their invitation. If needed, we will clear our calendars and reschedule other appointments to make time for them. Such a request to be in their company fills us with joy and excitement.

God is no different. He is passionate about His relationship with you, and He has made a way for you to draw close to Him. In fact, He went to great lengths to restore what was lost from the beginning. And because of the finished work of Christ Jesus, we can come boldly into His presence, without guilt, shame or condemnation.

Within the pages of Scripture, we find numerous invitations to draw closer to God and to seek Him while He may be found. The incredible invitation from the Creator of the universe is not just to worship Him from afar with words and rituals, but to enter a relationship so meaningful and intimate that you know His heart and He knows yours.

In *Nearer to God*, my friend Wayman Ming provides a road map that will guide you into the God chaser's greatest desire—the presence of God! This journey is not a matter of miles, but a matter of experience. And as you seek His nearness, you will find yourself treading on sacred ground. If you have been longing for a deeper relationship with God, then I am so excited that you're holding this book in your hands. Intimacy with God awaits you; now it is time to draw near.

John Bevere, bestselling author and minister;
co-founder, Messenger International

Acknowledgments

When authors write books, they sometimes feel like free-throw shooters at the end of a big basketball game. They step up to the line on the assumption that they will make the shot, but they are not quite sure. Somehow, we authors believe our book will make a difference, but there is always a question mark at the end of the sentence. If *Nearer to God—Closing the Distance between You and Your Creator* somehow impacts you, it certainly will have been enhanced by the following:

> To Him who is able to do exceedingly abundantly above all that we ask or think, according to the power that works in us, to Him be glory in the church by Christ Jesus to all generations.
>
> Ephesians 3:20–21

At the end of a movie, there is always a list of credits given to the behind-the-scenes people who helped in the production process. Big thank-yous to the following people who have helped me make the free-throw at the end of the big game:

To my wife, Kimberly, who encourages me all the time to live for an audience of One. (You have always inspired me to stand up and be counted whatever the cost.)

To my son Spencer, who is wise beyond his years. (You have the potential to shake nations with your words and pen. Simply hear God's voice and obey God's voice. Thank you for believing in your lifelong Coach.)

To my son Garrett, who has more talent in his little finger than I have in my entire body. (Always serve the Lord with humility and maintain a teachable spirit. God gives grace and blesses the humble. I love you, Vazu.)

To my daughter, Grace, who is the apple of her dad's eye. (You are my favorite girl. Thank you for inspiring me.)

To my mother, Karen Ming Kliewer, who lives vicariously through her children, grandchildren and great-grandchildren. (You will never understand how much of an inspiration you are to all of us. You have modeled prayer in our family and inspired us to become just like you when we grow up.)

To my brothers, Jared and Brian Ming, who are always there for me. (Thank you for inspiring me to enjoy the journey.)

To my father- and mother-in-law, Doyle and Shirley Thomlison. (You have always been a cup of cold water in a dry and weary land. Thank you for loving me as your son.)

1

Interrupting Life as Usual

Look! The virgin will conceive a child! She will give
birth to a son, and they will call him Immanuel,
which means "God is with us."

Matthew 1:23 NLT

In early 2020, the horrific consequences of COVID-19 impacted
everything! Very few of us ever anticipated a global lockdown.
Certainly even as business offices were closed and shelter-
in-place orders were given, no one in the community of faith
expected the closure of church gatherings. Yet, that is what
happened. For months, we remained sequestered in our homes
with no way to engage in church activities.

When the world came to a standstill, Christians of all ages
and stages of spiritual life were confronted with how they
had compartmentalized their faith. The "sometimes-show-up
Christians" took their spiritual temperature and realized that

attending church on Sunday while living for self on Monday could never sustain them in the midst of crisis. Opening the Bible sometimes and leaving it closed the rest of the time was only adding to their spiritual angst. Even the "always-show-up Christians" recognized that to engage in church activities was not the same as daily devotion to God. In fact for many of them, their attempt to be faithful by maintaining a full calendar of church events had only impeded their full pursuit of God.

Since God cares compassionately for the hurting, I certainly do not wish to minimize the tragedy of the circumstances surrounding COVID-19. However, I cannot help but wonder: What if God occasionally allows disasters in order to interrupt life as usual and begin a process of reforming His people? What if He uses tribulation in the world to remind us that the Church is not a building or a place but a *people* who pursue the person and presence of God? Stated simply, what if God allows divine interruptions to help close the distance between Him and His people?

My purpose in writing this book is not necessarily to offer a comprehensive discussion of the "why" behind disaster—why a gracious God would allow a pandemic like the coronavirus, or why a good God would allow pain and suffering. In fact, this book is not really about disaster at all. Instead, birthed out of a passion for drawing nearer to God, it is about how to *respond* in times of disaster.

Throughout history, God has interrupted life as usual with wakeup calls, beginning with Adam and Eve, when God interrupted their game of "hide-and-seek" in the bushes. During the time of Noah, "God took one look and saw how bad it was, everyone corrupt and corrupting—life itself corrupt to the core" (Genesis 6:12 MESSAGE) and decided to interrupt it with a flood. For Moses, divine interruption came through a burning bush. Abraham's effort to sacrifice his son was interrupted by a ram in the thicket. Throughout the era of the kings and prophets, culture and conquest were interrupted through supernatural signs and miraculous wonders. Then after four hundred years of silence during the intertestamental years, the ultimate interruption took place:

> Look! The virgin will conceive a child! She will give birth to a son, and they will call him Immanuel, which means "God is with us."
>
> Matthew 1:23 NLT (See also Galatians 4:4–5)

Humankind witnessed the most extravagant example of how God closed the distance—the coming of Immanuel, which means "God is with us."

From that moment on, the invitation for a personal relationship with God has remained at the forefront of God's mission on earth. For some, such as the disciples, Jesus simply shows up and invites them to leave everything behind and follow Him. Others, like Saul who would later become Paul, He abruptly knocks off their high horse into the dirt and calls for a radical change of purpose. Though Paul is an example of one who responded to God with a yes, many others, such as the rich young ruler, choose to walk away from Him. Regardless, in every case God has a reason for His divine interruption of life as usual.

As we look at the 21st century, I believe God is using chaotic circumstances, whether human-made (like 9/11) or naturally induced (such as the coronavirus or Hurricane Katrina), as opportunities for anyone and everyone to come closer to Him. To close the distance between ourselves and God, we must traverse a two-way street: The initial interruption belongs to Him, while the lifelong response belongs to us. As the Scripture declares, those who do not know God can seek and find Him if they search for Him with all their hearts (see Jeremiah 29:13).

Even those who already know Him must engage in the search. Pastors and church leaders must diligently seek Him. Christian organizations and denominations must intentionally embark on a pursuit of Him. God is eager and willing to close the distance with us if we are willing to close the distance with Him.

My family once had a garage sale, and one of the items we sold was my children's LEGO set. As preschoolers, my sons would construct grand creations that had no recognizable form. Only after Dad sat down and began to take the pieces apart and put them back together again did a purposeful piece of architecture take shape. As you read through the pages of *Nearer to God: Closing the Distance between You and Your Creator,* may our Dad in heaven begin to take the pieces of your life apart and put them back together again in a way that will help you understand both why life as usual has been interrupted and how to begin a sacred cooperation that will close the distance between yourself and Him.

Personal REFLECTION

Throughout history, God has interrupted life as usual with wakeup calls to close the distance with humankind. Often, the worst of times can serve as inspirational moments and become the best of times, especially when our attention is turned toward God. Allow this premise to launch you toward a brand-new journey of closing the distance between you and your Creator. Reflect on the following questions.

1. As you look back on your life, can you think of some specific events that seem to have been God's interruptions of your life as usual, designed to get your attention?

2. How did these past events attract you to God—or distract you from drawing nearer to Him?

3. How are current events attracting or distracting you as far as drawing nearer to God is concerned?

4. Reflect on the notion that closing the distance with God is really a two-way street: The initial interruption belongs to Him, while the lasting response belongs to you.

5. Are you willing to pursue God and to respond to Him?

Personal PRAYER

Heavenly Father, today I want to begin a journey to come nearer to You. I no longer want to settle for where I have been or even where I am right now. I want to go somewhere I have never been in my relationship with You. I want You to interrupt my "life as usual" and to close the distance between us. I want the circumstances of life to attract me toward You and not distract me away from You. Thank You for initiating the relationship. Now help me to engage in a lasting response. In the name of Your Son, Jesus, Amen.

Group CHALLENGE

Even though our journey toward God is extremely personal, we often find inspiration from those who travel on the same path. Allow your reflections concerning your own pursuit to encourage others in their pursuit. Here are some prompts:

1. As you reflect on your own decision to come nearer to God, what would you say to those who are considering the same decision?

2. At some point, people will decide to allow their chaotic circumstances, whether human-made or naturally induced, either to attract them toward God or to distract them away from God. Discuss this notion as a group.

3. Reflect on the idea that closing the distance with God is really a two-way street: The initial interruption belongs to Him, while the lasting response belongs to us.

4. Discuss the specific events in the past that you can now see have pointed to God interrupting "life as usual" to get your attention.

5. At the end of this chapter, you read the following statement: "Only after Dad sat down and began to take the pieces apart and put them back together again did a purposeful piece of architecture take shape." As a group, discuss the significance of this.

2

Find the GodFather

"For I know the plans I have for you," says the Lord.
"They are plans for good and not for disaster, to give
you a future and a hope."

Jeremiah 29:11 NLT

he Godfather film series remains one of the most well-known movie classics in American history. Initially, we are introduced to "Don" Vito Corleone, who is the head (godfather) of the Corleone mafia family in New York City. Through the twists and turns of the series, the infamous role of the "Don" and full control of the clandestine empire is transferred to his youngest son, Michael Corleone. In one of the more compelling plotlines of the third movie of *The Godfather* trilogy, Michael asks Kay, the love of his life, "Do you still fear me, Kay?" Her reply: "I don't fear you, Michael. I just dread you."[1]

Even though murder and criminal activity are presented as a way of life, one centripetal theme emerges—the godfather assumes full control, and he directs every chaotic event that occurs.

Now, no New York crime boss can be compared to the majesty and moral purity of the GodFather of heaven. Yet when people are struggling through anxiety, chaos, pain and devastation, some make the leap to draw parallels between the two. In such life-altering circumstances, it is not uncommon for the GodFather of heaven to be accused of acting like a villainous bully, blamed for every misdeed in the world as if He is like the Don of NYC.

God's Plans for Our Good

During times of crisis, fear and dread are often the unfortunate terms associated with God as He is blamed for whatever disaster disappoints the masses at the moment. However, as we begin to know the GodFather, we begin to recognize His true nature, and we learn to exchange our fear for His love and our dread for His peace. We begin to experience the reality of the Scripture that states: "And we have known and believed the love that God has for us. God is love, and he who abides in love abides in God, and God in him" (1 John 4:16).

In fact, when our hearts have been broken by the cares of life, God chooses to come even closer. As the psalmist declares: "The LORD is close to the brokenhearted; he rescues those whose spirits are crushed" (Psalm 34:18 NLT). In essence, God will use those brokenhearted and crushed moments in life to help us know who He really is.

One such moment occurred in the Old Testament when King Nebuchadnezzar had invaded Jerusalem. He did not fly airplanes into their World Trade Center or release a deadly virus to destroy the innocent, but he did invade homes, slaughter children and forcibly destroy their way of life. As Jerusalem was reduced to rubble, the local population witnessed the funeral of a city. Undoubtedly, they were discouraged and distraught. The entire book of Lamentations was written because of this devastation, and yet in the midst of their mess God inserted the prophetic voice of Jeremiah: "'For I know the plans I have for you,' says the LORD. 'They are plans for good and not for disaster, to give you a future and a hope'" (Jeremiah 29:11 NLT).

Mercifully, God built up the faith of His people in the midst of their dire circumstances, and He continues to do the same today. Whether we point to the collapse of the World Trade Center on 9/11 or look toward a post-COVID-19 world, we can see how God chooses to show up and inspire His people with His plans and purposes for their lives.

In 2011, one of the deadlier tornados in modern history, an EF5-rated multiple-vortex tornado, devastated the city where I lived—Joplin, Missouri. Countless individuals were touched by this one catastrophic event, as 158 people lost their lives, over one thousand were injured and properties were damaged in excess of 2.8 billion dollars.[2] Stories of compounded human tragedies were widespread: A friend told me about her neighbor, who was burned from the chest down when a water heater fell on top of her while she tried to protect herself in her bathtub. For twelve straight miles, the city of Joplin looked like a war zone.

For months afterward, our community of faith delivered food and supplies to families. One was a single mother who had lost everything except her two babies (one child was only a week old and the other a year and a half). But how could we address the spiritual and emotional needs?

When terrorism, plagues and disasters occur, all kinds of questions flood our minds, such as, "How could this happen?" "Is God really concerned about us?" "If God is such a loving Father, where is He in the midst of this?" C. S. Lewis once wrote, "God whispers to us in our pleasures, speaks in our conscience, but shouts in our pains: it is His megaphone to rouse a deaf world."[3] The truth is that our God chooses to embrace us through the midst of our suffering, and He reminds us that His plans are still good.

It is easier to make a powerful argument for the sovereignty of the GodFather—the idea that He is in absolute control—when everything around us is neat and orderly, but what about when things are in utter chaos? How do we cope when our world has been turned upside down?

Preoccupation Theology

"The sovereignty of God" sounds good in a Sunday sermon or Bible class, but what happens when a twelve-year-old girl wanders into a shelter with a broken jaw and a swollen face, having seen her mother crushed in a tornado? What are you supposed to think when you have your father or mother taken from you because of a deadly virus that started somewhere on the other side of the world? Yes, you can say or believe that God is still in control, but where is the evidence?

In the light of such circumstances, God can feel distant or even absent, and it is easy for our thoughts and beliefs to spiral toward the conclusion that He must be preoccupied or even disinterested. Some even claim that God created the world and set it into motion, thereby establishing the moral, natural and spiritual laws that govern it, but once the initial work was through, He then decided to passively watch from the sidelines, unconcerned about the details of human life. For those who adopt this deistic belief, God remains wholly transcendent and never immanent.

Unfortunately, "preoccupation theology" does not reconcile with God's continuing invitation to build a personal relationship with Him. If God is so far removed from the daily struggles of humankind, why bother praying to Him? Why should we seek Him or choose to follow Him if we have no real access to Him?

Actually, the closer we get to God, the more we learn that He has not withdrawn Himself from the mayhem of humankind or abandoned us on the doorstep of life to fend for ourselves. God is not up there in the celestial choir singing "Que sera sera."[4] Quite the opposite, God always responds with those life-giving words, "I know the plans I have for you. . . . They are plans for good and not disaster."

Puppeteer Theology

While some believe that God remains preoccupied or disinterested, others endorse the antithesis: They think that He is a type of "Master Puppeteer" who pulls the strings of our lives any way He desires. This ideology suggests that nothing in life occurs without God's direct involvement and that He seeks to control our every decision, such as putting on a ball cap or squeezing toothpaste in the middle of the tube or determining every win or loss for the local high school football team. This idealistic worldview in which God coerces humankind to abide by His whimsical idiosyncrasies also requires Him to take full responsibility for every disaster and history-altering event. Paradoxically, this brand of theology gives people a world where they not only are no longer at fault but also have hung themselves up like puppets on imaginary strings.

Such a belief creates more tension than resolution because it does not offer a satisfactory explanation for the effects of bad decisions. If God is involved in *every* decision, why does He not keep us from making mistakes or stop us from sinning against Him or others? Why does He not stop airplanes from flying into towers or viruses from killing innocent people? Why does He not stop bad things from happening to good people?

While "preoccupation theology" does not encourage the development of a personal relationship with God, "puppeteer theology" does not promote the development of a free moral will. Though God is sovereign and does exercise a measure of control and power over the world, we can be thankful that we exist as more than just puppets on a string. Because of the depth of His love and desire for us to grow into His virtue, He allows us to make choices and decisions, whether they are good or bad. God does not choose your ball cap; you do. God does not choose where you squeeze the toothpaste; you do. And God does not determine who wins or loses the football game; the players do. Whether the world seems to be upside down or right side up, God still remains good, and He allows us to exist with a free moral will.

Perhaps we need a more credible headline, something like, "God Creates the Human Brain to Be Used." Why would God create the human mind, with all of its uniqueness and complexity, if He intended to make all of our decisions for us? We know that parents who make all of the decisions for their children and never allow them to act on their own inevitably doom them to a life of immaturity and failure. We should be glad that the GodFather remains committed to our maturity and success, and that He allows us to walk through a full human experience, one that includes both success and failure. Any other plan for human life would fall short of providing the conditions necessary for healthy growth and a good future.

God's Plans for Our Future

The fact is, the city of Jerusalem had already lost her future long before Nebuchadnezzar's invasion took place. One might think that the children of Israel lost sight of their future only after the invasion, but the record in the book of Lamentations reveals otherwise:

> She [Jerusalem] defiled herself with immorality and *gave no thought to her future.* Now she lies in the gutter with no one to lift her out. "Lᴏʀᴅ, see my misery," she cries. "The enemy has triumphed."
>
> Lamentations 1:9 ɴʟᴛ, emphasis added

How often do we do the same, blaming God for a future we have already relinquished ourselves? Why do we tend to pin the problem on God when human choices are at fault?

My wife and I used to watch the television drama *Chicago Fire*, even though, like most shows, it did not necessarily present an accurate biblical picture of the nature of God. In one episode, a helicopter crashed into a residential area, pinning a poor woman underneath a detached propeller blade. The firefighter who responded to the emergency call made the following observation: "It was like the hand of God dropped this propeller on this woman."

Obviously God does not drop propellers on people, and more specifically, God does not injure and harm people. It is important to note that God does not administer the beatings in life at all. Jesus Himself declared: *"The thief's* [Satan's] *purpose is to steal and kill and destroy.* My purpose is to give them a rich and satisfying life" (John 10:10 ɴʟᴛ, emphasis added). We sometimes forget that it is the enemy of our soul who seeks to ravage the world with destruction.

The word *steal* here is translated from the Greek word *klepto*, which is the root for the word *kleptomania*. A kleptomaniac is someone who impulsively takes things without a reason; stealing is a component of a kleptomaniac's nature. The point is this: Since Scripture effectively describes Satan as a kleptomaniac, then we have to acknowledge that by nature he has no moral compass. He steals from us without remorse or conscience.

Furthermore, Satan is a killer, and we know that the word *kill* means "to slaughter" or "to cut up in little pieces." Satan intends not only to hurt people, but also to annihilate them. Scripture tells us that Satan's purpose includes our destruction. Satan wants to see us ruined. He is fixated on the goal of rendering us unusable. He wants to destroy us to the point that we are no longer profitable or productive to ourselves or anyone else.

Thankfully, the movie that God is directing does not end here. Bad endings may work on occasion for movies, fiction or fairy tales, but they do not work for real believers. Christians are real people with real problems, and we follow a real God—who writes real good endings. Our lives may not always feel "happily ever after," but with God there is always something good waiting around the corner.

Satan may continue to seek to push the world toward gross darkness, but the Church is in the way, and the Church does not operate on the defensive but rather on the offensive. In fact, the Church should not be spending too much time trying to stop hell from invading. Instead, hell should be trying to stop the Church. Who is stopping whom? It depends upon our enlistment status. In other words, if hell is stopping us, then we are not fighting in the army of the Lord or building what He is building. Remember that Jesus said, "I will build my church, and all the powers of hell will not conquer it" (see Matthew 16:18 NLT).

In the very first prophecy of the Bible, God declared that Satan may bruise the woman's heel but that he would receive a crushed head in the process (see Genesis 3:15). When it draws nearer to God, the Church stops playing the role of the crushed head and begins to play the role of the bruised heel. We may experience some bruising along the way, but we are still the ones doing the crushing. We are still on the best side of Jesus' promise: "The thief's [Satan's] purpose is to steal and kill and destroy. My purpose is to give them a rich and satisfying life" (John 10:10 NLT).

I wonder how often we emphasize the first part of that verse and neglect the latter half. Especially when bad things begin to happen, God seems to get only the negative press, even when human choice or evil engagement remains part of the equation. When a helicopter crashes, should the blame rest with God or with pilot or mechanical error? If someone's car is repossessed, is God at fault for failure to make the car payment? How can the dark presence of a sinister evil be attributed to the light?

Like a press anchorman, Jesus actually addresses this: He provides some accurate news coverage of two community disasters. The first involved Pilate and the Galileans. Galilee was the home region of a group of Zealots who were committed to the overthrow of the Roman government. When Pilate, the Roman governor, heard about their plot, he instigated a preemptive strike to kill the Galileans while they were offering their sacrifices in the Temple. Many Jews believed that when terrible events occurred, the consequences were deserved—the eye-for-an-eye and tooth-for-a-tooth principle. In other words, the Galileans deserved to die because they were guilty of plotting against Rome, and they must have been worse sinners than other citizens. Jesus debunks this idea, remarking, "Do you think those Galileans were worse sinners than all the other people from Galilee? . . . Is that why they suffered? Not at all!" (Luke 13:2–3 NLT). Imagine the gasps in the crowd when Jesus refuted their understanding. He shifted their paradigm: Bad things do not happen only to the worst sinners. Bad things happen because sin exists.

Simply stated, the problem is sin. We live in an imperfect world filled with imperfect people who are involved in imperfect situations. Horrific and heartbreaking tragedies occur every day. A wife receives a black eye from her husband. A child is hit and killed by a drunk driver. An innocent man receives a life sentence in prison. Such situations may cause us to become incensed with injustice, but we should not blame God. He is not the one who threw the punch, drove the vehicle while intoxicated or committed the crime. People make horrible decisions that affect others, and evil is real. If we believe that God is always dropping propellers on humankind, we will forget that His purpose for us is not disaster and destruction, but rather a promising future.

In the second "news" story of Luke 13, Jesus changes the focus from sinful human actions to a natural disaster. A famous tower in Jerusalem had given way and toppled over, and it had crushed eighteen people to death. Unlike the first news report, in which people were slaughtered by an act of human aggression, the second report spoke of a tragedy in which people were killed simply by being in the wrong place at the wrong time.

> And what about the eighteen people who died when the tower in Siloam fell on them? Were they the worst sinners in Jerusalem? No, and I tell you again that unless you repent, you will perish, too.
>
> Luke 13:4–5 NLT

Does this sound familiar? A tornado, hurricane or earthquake devastates a city or nation. A deadly virus touches the lives of countless millions.

When Hurricane Katrina slammed into New Orleans, Louisiana in 2005, 2,000 people died and over 1 million people were displaced from their homes.[5] Sad to say, some people declared, "The city of New Orleans is getting what it deserves—God's judgment on a wicked city." Then they gave a litany of biblical examples to justify how God apparently uses natural disasters to judge sin, such as the worldwide flood, the ten plagues of Egypt and the destruction of Sodom and Gomorrah.

Interestingly, these same people neglected to mention that the righteous were actually saved in each of these examples.

Noah and his family were saved on the ark. The children of Israel walked away from the bonds of slavery, and Lot and his daughters escaped without even smelling like smoke.

Those of us who find the GodFather recognize that He is not toppling towers on people or sending hurricanes to judge the worst sinners among us. Actually, He always seeks to do the opposite. He is a loving Father who has good plans for our future and hope.

God's Plans for Our Hope

It is interesting to note that Jeremiah inserted the word *future* before the word *hope*. Perhaps it is because our future inspires our hope. When we can see something, we can conceive something. When we can see a future, we can conceive a hope.

However, hope tends to be elusive, especially when the circumstances of life remain difficult. Where was hope when the priests, prophets and citizens of Jerusalem were kidnapped from their homes and taken to another nation during Nebuchadnezzar's invasion? In their dispersion and exile, the Jewish people did not need to endure only a few weeks of pain and sorrow; they had to endure seventy devastating years as captives in a strange land.

In the midst of suffering, people tend to lose hope. Their hope has been disappointed, and this development has produced a sickness that cannot easily be remedied. The writer of Proverbs addressed the situation: "Hope deferred makes the heart sick, but when the desire comes, it is a tree of life" (Proverbs 13:12).

Notice that deferred hope produces heartache. In other words, lost hope results in lost health. Let me restate the obvious: Hopeful people are healthy people. To possess hope, an "inward expectation concerning a better future" creates positive movement

31

toward a desired destination. It is a game changer. No wonder God connects our future and hope together.

Even faith depends upon our willingness to engage in hope: "Now faith is the substance of things hoped for, the evidence of things not seen" (Hebrews 11:1). That is to say, God's unseen substance is revealed through the expectation of our hope. One of the greatest weapons available to help us overcome the chaos of life remains our hope—our hope in God. The psalmist David knew this. He wrote, "Why am I discouraged? Why is my heart so sad? I will put my hope in God! I will praise him again—my Savior and my God!" (Psalm 42:5–6 NLT).

To be sure, we should place our hope not in ourselves or even in others, but in God! We can do our very best to overcome our discouragement through human effort, but we will never be able to save ourselves. A hole will remain in our soul. A praying spouse or family member will not be able to deliver us. Coaches and care-providers cannot provide ultimate healing. Whenever a crisis occurs or another horrific tragedy flashes across the screen of our lives, our hope must be placed in God.

If we do not put our hope in God, we will become angry and bitter, like the Jewish people during the Babylonian captivity. We will grumble, "Why is the government not prepared? Why are our government agencies not responding? Where is God in the midst of this?" Yet the truth remains: God is not missing in action. Despite our feelings, He is in fact closer at that moment of despair than He ever was before. He doesn't want to use our difficulties to arrest our hope, but rather to reinforce it.

If my young son takes a walk beside me and he happens to trip and fall down, is that my fault? Obviously not. And although I did not cause his fall, I will be swift to pick him up and hold him until he stops crying. In much the same way, there will be times when you will be walking beside your heavenly GodFather, and unexpectedly you will trip and fall down. Will your fall be His fault? Of course not. But His response will always be the same. He will reach down and pick you up until you stop crying, and while He comforts you, He will remind you:

> "I will never fail you. I will never abandon you."
>
> Hebrews 13:5 NLT

> "I have told you all this so that you may have peace in me. Here on earth you will have many trials and sorrows. But take heart, because I have overcome the world."
>
> John 16:33 NLT

> "Come to me, all of you who are weary and carry heavy burdens, and I will give you rest."
>
> Matthew 11:28 NLT

When we genuinely find the GodFather, we will be able to exchange our pain for His presence. Pain is a small word with a strong hold, but His love is greater. We will *find* Him; we will recognize that He is always with us. He will always provide peace in the midst of our sorrows and rest despite our heavy burdens.

In *The Godfather* trilogy, the most well-known quotation is actually spoken by both Vito and Michael Corleone during their respective times of leadership: "I'm gonna make him an offer he can't refuse."[6] Of course, the Corleone empire had amassed so much wealth and power—sometimes expressed by means of a gun to the head—that an offer was never easily refused. Thankfully, the GodFather of heaven does not make such vague or threatening offers. His offers are always for our good, our future and our hope. Now, truly those are offers we cannot refuse!

Personal CHALLENGE

The more you find the real GodFather, the more you will know His plans for your life. Relationship *with* Him results in revelation *from* Him. Notice the proper sequence: Finding God results in knowing His plans. How often do we miss out on His plans because we are seeking to know the plans rather than the Giver of the plans?

In a stunning profession of faith, the apostle Paul declared, "And my God shall supply all your need according to His riches in glory by Christ Jesus" (Philippians 4:19). Paul expressed the personal nature of His relationship with his Father God emphatically—"*my* God." In essence, Paul's personal connection with God supplied everything he needed, and it will do the same for you and for me.

When your mission is clear, your response is simple. So here is your mission: Make a definite decision to find God. When you pursue Him with passion, you will not have to worry about how to discover His good plans for your life. Finding and knowing the GodFather will embody your future with hope.

Personal REFLECTION

Despite and even by means of dire circumstances, God intends to build His relationship with each of His people. Even in the worst times, such as the collapse of the World Trade Center in 2001 or the COVID-19 world of 2020–2021, God chooses to show up. When they turn to Him, His people can be inspired as He lays out His plans and purposes for their lives. Allow the lessons you have learned in this chapter to motivate you to evaluate your own relationship with your heavenly GodFather.

1. At some point, most of us come face-to-face with the identity and nature of the GodFather. How do you relate to this? What are your reflections?

2. Past tragedies may have caused you to lose hope in God, others and yourself. What specific tragedies of the past may have caused you to blame God, others or yourself?

3. Take a look at your own heart. Do you see signs of "deferred hope"? If so, what do they look like?

4. On the flip side, do you see signs of God's plans for your good, your future and your hope? If so, what are these signs?

5. Are you willing to open up your heart to the GodFather so that you can pursue Him as never before? What areas of your heart might be restricting you from doing so?

Personal PRAYER

Heavenly Father, I am praying to find and to know the real God-Father. Forgive me for blaming You for the disasters created by the decisions of others or by the destructiveness of the enemy. I recognize that You are here for my good, my future and my hope. I intentionally place my hope in You so that it will not be "deferred hope" that produces heart sickness. I expect it to grow into an authentic hope that is inspired by knowing You. I want to have a healthy relationship with You as my GodFather. Amen.

Group CHALLENGE

The Jewish people of the dispersion ended up living through a nightmare in a strange land. Although they had lost everything,

God showed up and declared His plans for their good, their future and their hope. Allow your reflections about God's response in the midst of their crisis to initiate a group discussion. Here are some prompts:

1. As you have reflected (above, under Personal Reflection) with regard to your own confrontation with the identity and nature of the GodFather, what can you share with the others in the group?

2. Share your reflections about the C. S. Lewis quote: "God whispers to us in our pleasures, speaks in our conscience, but shouts in our pains: it is His megaphone to rouse a deaf world."[7]

3. At some point, many Christians confront the betrayal barrier, which they come up against when they think they have been betrayed by God or that He is not really interested in where they are. Discuss this notion as a group.

4. Discuss your views with regard to the following:
   a. Preoccupation Theology—the idea that God is removed from the daily struggles of humankind
   b. Puppeteer Theology—the idea that God is overly involved in the daily decisions of humankind

5. Now that you have read about the plans of God, are you willing to open up your heart to the GodFather and pursue Him as never before? Examine your heart and mind. What might restrict you from doing so?

3

Follow the Real Rock Star

> He [Jesus] said to them, "But who do you say that I am?" Simon Peter answered and said, "You are the Christ, the Son of the living God."
>
> Matthew 16:15–16

Though I myself prefer the sounds of classic '80s love songs and artists such as Journey and Phil Collins, superstars like Beyoncé have captured the hearts and the attention of billions around the globe. At one particular show in 2011 (Glastonbury, England), which has been identified by *Billboard* magazine as the third greatest festival performance of all time, a secretly three-months-pregnant Beyoncé made her entrance onto a pyramid stage via hydraulic platform, with fireworks.[1] She delighted the audience with favorites such as "Single Ladies (Put a Ring on It)" and "Halo" and sang cover hits such as Etta James' "At Last," and then she expressed the following sentiment: "You are witnessing a dream! I always wanted to be a rock star."[2] The audience that night endorsed her every word.

Many people are enthralled by the glitz and glamor of Hollywood's latest and greatest on the stage. Over the years, reality talent shows like *American Idol*, *America's Got Talent* and *The Voice* have reinforced a rock star culture. When asked the question "Why did you come on the show?" contestants from all over the globe will often respond, "This is my dream." The unsaid implication, of course, is nearly always a personal ambition of fame; they want to become the next Steve Perry, Beyoncé or another entertainer who currently enraptures a worldwide audience.

The dream of stardom may be appropriate in the entertainment industry, with its spotlights and applause. But in the context of the Christian Church, "spotlight ministry" proves to be incongruous and out of place. When John the Baptist was pressed to take the stage during Jesus' day, he emphatically declined, saying, "He must increase, and I must decrease." Or as the New Living Translation puts it, "He must become greater and greater, and I must become less and less" (John 3:30 NLT). Simply stated, there can only be one real Rock Star here—Jesus Christ.

In the New Testament, the apostle Peter echoes an ancient declaration given by God to the prophet Isaiah: "Behold, I lay in Zion a chief cornerstone, elect, precious, and he who believes on Him will by no means be put to shame" (1 Peter 2:6). Then Paul reinforced this when he wrote: "All of them [the Israelites] ate the same spiritual food, and all of them drank the same spiritual water. For they drank from the spiritual rock that traveled with them, and that rock was Christ" (1 Corinthians 10:3–4 NLT).

Spotlight ministry, of course, is not a new problem in the Church. As early as the first century, it had already made an impact on the church in Corinth. The apostle Paul swiftly addressed it:

> I appeal to you, dear brothers and sisters, by the authority of our Lord Jesus Christ, to live in harmony with each other. Let there be no divisions in the church. Rather, be of one mind, united in thought and purpose. For some members of Chloe's household have told me about your quarrels, my dear brothers and sisters. *Some of you are saying, "I am a follower of Paul." Others are saying, "I follow Apollos," or "I follow Peter," or "I follow only Christ."* Has Christ been divided into factions? Was I, Paul, crucified for you? Were any of you baptized in the name of Paul?
>
> 1 Corinthians 1:10–13 NLT, emphasis added

Some of the early Christians were lining up behind their favorite personalities, which caused Paul to reiterate the importance of following Christ above any other leader, and that included even himself. All of us know enough about Church culture to be able to imagine the kinds of things those Corinthian believers must have been saying: "You should hear Apollos preach. He can really bring it." "Oh yeah, what about Peter? Have you heard his fishing illustrations?" As a consequence, Jesus Christ ended up as merely one "personality" among many.

A rock star culture within the Church will always stand diametrically opposed to the heart of God, and it will always widen the spiritual distance between Him and His people.

Following Christ

The greatest divine interruption in history occurred when "God so loved the world that He gave His only begotten Son, that whoever believes in Him should not perish but have everlasting life" (John 3:16). In that moment, humankind witnessed God's ultimate commitment to close the spiritual distance—the gift of His Son to the world for all generations. Yet His gift has not always been received, as many have struggled to accept and follow Him.

Do you remember when Jesus asked His disciples the question, "Who do you say that I am?" (Matthew 16:15). He was addressing the most important question of all time—Who *is* Jesus? God will continue to interrupt our lives with that question until we answer it with clarity. He is 100 percent committed to closing the distance between Himself and us.

I have personally traveled to Israel and visited the approximate place where Jesus asked this question. Back in the first century, the location was called Caesarea Philippi, so named because the Romans had erected a large temple dedicated to Caesar Philip. In addition, approximately fourteen other temples peppered the landscape in honor of the Syrian god Baal, and a large temple built for the god Pan could be seen there. With this pantheistic and polytheistic backdrop of diverse temples to diverse gods, Jesus asked the question, "Who do you say that I am?"[3]

If we dig into the text, we might notice a translation challenge in the word *you*. ("Who do *you* say that I am?") In the original Greek text, *you* is plural, but in English, there is no proper way to attribute plurality to second-person pronouns. Actually, American Southerners have resolved the issue. They have come up with a better English translation of the text: "Who do y'all say that I am?" All kidding aside, the point is this: Jesus' question is not asked to an individual disciple but to all the disciples. Therefore, when Peter speaks up, he does not reply for himself only but also on behalf of the whole group. "You are the Christ, the Son of the living God" (Matthew 16:16).

It is worth noting that this story did not happen at the beginning of Jesus' ministry. In fact, by this point the disciples had already traveled and lived with Him for over a year. They had already heard the Sermon on the Mount and watched Him perform many miracles. They had heard Him refer to Himself as the Son of Man many times. The term *Son of Man* is significant for several reasons. Not only was it Jesus' favorite title for Himself—He called Himself the Son of Man at least 81 times—but it was an Old Testament reference that Jesus' Jewish disciples would not have missed:

> I was watching in the night visions, and behold, One like the Son of Man, coming with the clouds of heaven! He came to the Ancient of Days, and they brought Him near before Him. Then to Him was given dominion and glory and a kingdom, that all peoples, nations, and languages should serve Him. His dominion *is* an everlasting dominion, which shall not pass away, and His kingdom the one which shall not be destroyed.
>
> Daniel 7:13–14

Before Jesus posed this question to the disciples, some believed that He was the Messiah but not the Son of God. Consequently, when Simon Peter responded, "You are the Christ, the Son of the living God," he was identifying Jesus as the Messiah (Christ) and as deity (Son of God) all in the same sentence. This is the first recorded moment when Jesus' deity was affirmed!

Immediately after this, Jesus mentions the Church for the first time in these five words, "I will build My church" (Matthew 16:18). During the first century, the word *church* was a secular term that referred to any assembly of people; today it is a religious term. Yet it has always meant a body of people and not a building. So when Jesus says He will build His Church, He does not mean He will design and build a structure, but that He will build a body of people.

41

Jesus' statement, "I will build My church" is recorded in three of the four gospels, and in each instance it is stated in the same paragraph as Simon Peter's profession, "You are the Christ, the Son of the living God." It is profoundly significant to find that the first mention of the "church" is directly connected to Simon Peter's profession of Jesus' Lordship.

Why did Jesus wait all this time to mention the Church? He had already performed significant miracles, and He had shared profound wisdom with people in many places. I believe He waited to mention the Church until He had been proclaimed as Lord. To this day, there can be no Church unless Jesus Christ is Lord. Until He is the Ruling Authority who builds His Church, the Church does not exist.

Furthermore, the scriptural construct of Jesus' words is pre-emptive in that He uses two personal pronouns within the five words: "I" and "My." "*I* will build *My* church." This is true even if the sentence is restructured to read, "This is *My* church, and *I* will build it." In other words, there is no room for anyone else. To this day, when people succumb to the elevation and adulation of Christian celebrities and charismatic personalities, Jesus asserts Himself as the only real Rock Star.

Now in some Christian traditions, particularly Roman Catholicism, the apostle Peter is known as the rock of the Church. After all, the entire statement actually reads, "You are Peter, and on this rock I will build My church" (Matthew 16:18). Certainly Peter had spoken out on behalf of the disciples, because he led the pack. In fact, wherever you see a list of disciples in the gospels, Peter's name appears at the top. He is the spokesperson for the group, the one who preaches the first message and opens the doors of the first church. In light of early Church history, there is little doubt that Jesus identified Peter as a primary leader in His Church.

However, as we reconsider the current rock star culture in this chapter, we must remain cautious of the idea that Jesus wanted Peter to assume an elevated status. To allow Peter to take such preeminence in the Church would only distract from the One who deserves all the praise. I do not believe that Jesus intended to make Peter so important. When we look at the Greek text, we can get a better clue as to what Jesus might have meant. The word for "Peter" here is *petros* or stone, which is singular, but the Greek word for "rock" is *petra*—plural. Therefore a more true and accurate reading might result in an interpretation like this: "Peter, you are a stone, and upon many stones, I will build My Church." In other words, Jesus identifies Peter as one stone (singular) within the collective many stones (plural) that would be used to build His Church. Peter is certainly a rock, even an important rock at that, but by no means is he the true Rock Star.

God's comprehensive Kingdom cannot be built on one leader, one preacher or one spokesperson. It must be built upon the declaration, "You are the Christ, the Son of the living God."

Following the Christ-Life

At this point, Jesus begins to teach His disciples how to close the distance with Him. He shares:

> "If anyone desires to come after Me, let him deny himself, and take up his cross, and follow Me. For whoever desires to save his life will lose it, but whoever loses his life for My sake will find it. For what profit is it to a man if he gains the whole world, and loses his own soul? Or what will a man give in exchange for his soul?"
>
> Matthew 16:24–26

Initially Jesus had asked the question, "Who am I?" Now He asks, "Will you follow Me?"

Will *you* follow the Christ-life? This is the crux and crucible of the Christian faith. Are you willing to deny yourself, take up your cross and follow Him?

Speaking candidly, I have struggled with Jesus' challenge to "deny myself and take up my cross" at times because it seems like such a big assignment. It sounds impossible! Of course, you may hear people say, "My sickness is my cross," or, "My boss is my cross," but I do not think that this is what Jesus was talking about. Is it possible that some of us only want the attention that comes along with cross-carrying? Or is it possible that the crosses we think we bear are only Styrofoam replicas of those rough and weighty beams that were strapped across the back of our Savior?

Jesus' cross cost Him His life, and His words, "Take up your cross and follow Me" invite each of us to die as well.

Certainly we can experience cross-like situations that include serious illness, persecution and loss. But our real cross remains the same as Jesus' own; we must deny ourselves and follow Him. We sometimes think the problem is other people, but it is usually ourselves. Although we may believe that other people are the source of our unhappiness, the underlying source of our discontent is most often "self."

"Self" seeks to make the rules, call the shots and step into the spotlight. It acts like a toddler who says, "I do it my*self*," only to proceed to put on his shirt backward and tie his shoestrings together.

What comprises your "self"? I would suggest that it includes your mind (what you think), your will (what you want) and your emotions (how you feel). This is important to know, because "self" is often the deciding vote in the meeting that determines the way you live your life.

As three-part beings, all of us exist with a body, soul (self) and spirit. Since the body is associated with the physical realm and the spirit connects with the spiritual realm, then the deciding vote for most decisions is often left to the soul. Unfortunately, the soul (or self) has a strong tendency to align itself with the body (the physical realm), and this only increases our distance from God. But whenever your soul casts the deciding vote to deny its natural ("self-ish") inclination and instead to follow Christ, then you close the distance between yourself and God; you draw nearer to Him.

Ultimately, the assignment, "Deny yourself and follow Christ" is really about giving up your preference to live as the rock star of your own life in order that He might assume the lead role.

A Support Role, Not the Lead Role

When I was in college, I decided to audition for the role of Professor Harold Hill, the lead role in the musical *The Music Man*. Although I could have auditioned for a lesser role, I went after the spotlight. For months after I was eventually cast for the role, I learned my lines, ("Ah, you got trouble, right here in River City. . . .") and rehearsed songs such as "Seventy-Six Trombones" and "Marian the Librarian."

The week of performances eventually came off with great success, and I certainly found the curtain calls with applause to be affirming. But afterward I realized that the best part of the production had not been playing the lead role but rather the collaboration with my fellow cast members in the musical.

This principle readily applies to our spiritual journey. Jesus Christ plays the leading role, while we play various roles in the supporting cast. In simple terms, we do not have to "play God." Is that not refreshing and liberating? When we allow God to play the lead role, we are liberated from the overwhelming pressure of facing life on our own.

For many years, my family lived in southwest Missouri near the entertainment city of Branson, which is located in the Ozark Mountains (which are really more like hills) and is known for its family atmosphere. Although Branson holds a population of approximately ten thousand people, it hosts close to eight million tourists each year because of all the family entertainment.

It even has an amusement park—Silver Dollar City. My family would sometimes purchase annual passes to the park just so we could have access to the food, which includes barbecue chicken, grilled corn on the cob and funnel cakes. The park also provides game rooms and arcades where we could win stuffed animals and prizes by playing basketball or Whac-A-Mole.

Speaking of Whac-A-Mole, I always had a lot of fun with that mallet; but I was often frustrated because just about the time you would manage to hit the head of one of those little critters, another head would pop up. This is all too similar to daily life, where we find ourselves whacking down on one problem only to see another one emerging. One relational conflict gives way to another; one emotional crisis scarcely gets resolved before another one overwhelms us. We may walk around pretending that we are in control—"See here? I have the mallet!"—but we are not. If we were really in control, why then do we feel so frustrated and overwhelmed by the problems that continually pop up? If we are so all-powerful, why do we not just unplug the machine and stop the game? In reality, the only real solution is to relinquish control to Christ. We must do what He said: deny ourselves, take up our cross and follow Him.

A Relationship, Not a Religion

In our pursuit of the Christ-life, we must continually seek out a personal relationship with the Lord Jesus Christ instead of engaging in one religious activity after another. The theologian Henry Blackaby wrote,

> Knowing God does not come through a program or a method. It is a relationship with a Person. It is an intimate love relationship with God. Through this relationship, God reveals His will and invites you to join Him.[4]

Unfortunately, too many people confuse religion with relationship. They will attend church and hear Jesus' words on Sunday but have little regard for them on Monday. Or they will fulfill their Christian duty during special occasions but display no Christian discipline the rest of the year.

Remember the words of folk wisdom: "Just because you are in a garage, that don't make you a car. Just because you are in a barn, that don't make you a donkey. Just because you stick your head in an oven, that don't make you a chocolate cake. Just because you are in a McDonald's, that don't make you a Big Mac. And just because you attend church, that don't make you a Christian." The litmus test of your Christianity will never be your religious activity but always your personal relationship with Jesus Christ.

And while your relationship with Jesus may bring you great joy, it remains a serious commitment. Immediately after Jesus said, "If anyone desires to come after Me, let him deny himself, and take up his cross, and follow Me" (Matthew 16:24), He shared, "For whoever desires to save his life will lose it, but whoever loses his life for My sake will find it" (Matthew 16:25). Does losing your life for His sake sound like a casual commitment?

Regrettably, we are living in a culture that seems to take Christ casually. It is almost like people want to purchase Him for half price. You have seen the signs for storewide sales. Retail stores rely on the obvious fact that people do not want to pay full price when they can find something on sale. But we will never find Him on sale.

For the most part, the only time of year that I enjoy shopping is Christmas. I will frequent several stores and wander around in search of the one item that seems just right for my wife and each of my kids. One year, I shopped around until I found this fluffy white robe for my wife, Kimberly, and a pair of beautiful brown boots for my daughter, Grace. Usually I only know I have been successful when I see my gifts actually get used after Christmas, but on this particular shopping excursion, I already knew I had chosen well. To put the bow on top, I had purchased both items on sale.

Even though I like a sale price as much as the next person, I am eternally grateful that Jesus Christ cannot be purchased on sale. We have to pay full price, deny ourselves, take up our cross and follow Him. We have to decide to lose our life for His sake to find Him. As Jesus reminded us, absolute and wholehearted commitment is God's primary commandment to us: "'You shall love the LORD your God with all your heart, with all your soul, with all your mind, and with all your strength.' This is the first commandment" (Mark 12:30). The Christ-life carries with it a level of commitment that engages our entire being.

The psalmist said, "Blessed is everyone who fears the LORD, who walks in His ways" (Psalm 128:1). Naturally, "fear" tends to have a negative connotation, but in this context, fear really means "taking God seriously." Yes, fear may cause you to tremble because you are frightened, but the fear of the Lord really means that you hold Him in the highest esteem. From Psalm 128 we learn that our lives will be blessed when we take the Lord seriously and walk in His ways.

This may not be the most perfect example, but recently I was driving a bit too fast, and I saw a police car parked along the side of the highway. Immediately, I looked down at my speedometer to check my speed, and when I realized how fast I was going, I changed my footwork. The unseen police officer greatly affected my driving, and just knowing he was there influenced my decision-making instantly. I took the police car seriously, not casually. In a similar way, I have learned that when I take the Lord Jesus seriously, I will walk in His ways.

Because I am a pastor, I have had people come up to me at times a bit apologetically (and also somewhat defensively) saying, "I am not a religious person." I enjoy responding, "I'm not into religion either; I'm into a relationship with Jesus Christ."

The Christ-life is not about religion; it is about *relationship.*

A Character Call, Not a Curtain Call

At festivals or concerts, crowds have come to expect a "curtain call." At the end of a show, the crowd will cheer and applaud until the performers return to the stage to be recognized for their artistic excellence. This can sometimes take a while, especially for the finest performers, who receive the loudest and longest ovations. Trivia tidbit: The record for the longest curtain call in history is retained by Luciano Pavarotti, who on February 24, 1988, returned to the stage 165 times to be lauded for his performance in the Donizetti opera *L'Elisir D'Amore* at the Deutsche Oper Berlin. On this memorable evening, the audience applauded him for one hour and seven minutes.[5]

Certainly curtain calls are fine in the theater, but in the Church we Christians, and especially those of us who are Christian leaders, must not succumb to the lure of spotlight ministry. Never forget what Jesus said to His disciples after He taught about the importance of denying yourself and following Him. He said, "For what profit is it to a man if he gains the whole world, and loses his own soul? Or what will a man give in exchange for his soul?" (Matthew 16:26). The stakes are higher than we think.

Perhaps you have heard the story of the man who called a church's office and said, "I want to talk to the Head Hog at the Trough." After catching her breath, the secretary responded, "You may call him Pastor but not the Head Hog at the Trough." The man then continued, "That's fine, but I was thinking about making a one-hundred-thousand-dollar donation to the church." At which point she pivoted and responded, "Well, hold on for a moment; I think Porky just walked in the door."

Sadly, Christians, and especially Church leaders, will always be confronted with temptations to lose or exchange their souls for personal gain, but the call to value godly character remains the same. Remember the testimony of the apostle Paul, who had achieved much success as a Pharisee before Jesus Christ called him:

> I have been crucified with Christ; it is no longer I who live, but Christ lives in me; and the life which I now live in the flesh I live by faith in the Son of God, who loved me and gave Himself for me.
>
> Galatians 2:20

His reflection acknowledges the power of inward change. A couple of chapters later, he expands upon this idea: "My little children, for whom I labor in birth again until Christ is formed in you" (Galatians 4:19).

As we draw nearer to God, we always experience the reformative work of Christ from within. Called into Christ's classroom of character, we say together, "Professor Jesus, I'm here to learn from You. I want to pattern my life after Your life. I want to speak like You speak, live like You live and love like You love." Simply stated, when we follow the Christ-life, we stop looking for a curtain call and start hearing a *character* call.

When Nelson Mandela turned seventy, a rock concert was held in his honor at Wembley Stadium in the UK. Seventy thousand people piled into the stands to hear Guns N' Roses and numerous other rock bands. The event went on for twelve straight hours, and the raucous crowd freely imbibed alcohol and drugs. At the end of the concert, the final performer was an unknown artist, who walked out on stage without fanfare. With no instrumentation, she began to sing softly:

> Amazing grace, how sweet the sound
> That saved a wretch like me.
> I once was lost but now am found,
> Was blind, but now I see.

No one could have anticipated what happened next. A quiet hush fell over the stadium, and many in attendance started singing along with Jessye Norman to the tune of "Amazing Grace."[6] A raucous crowd had come to see all their favorite rock stars that day, and suddenly they had experienced a divine interruption. Unexpectedly, they found themselves exalting the real Rock Star—Jesus Christ. It is not too much to think that some may even have uttered a declaration like Simon Peter's: "You are the Christ, the Son of the living God."

Each one of us must speak those words for ourselves, from the heart.

Personal CHALLENGE

Because we too often succumb to the temptation to follow Christian celebrities and charismatic personalities, we need to be reminded that Jesus is the real Rock Star. As you reflect upon the challenges presented in this chapter, filter every consideration through the same grid. Ask yourself: "Does this keep Jesus Christ on the throne of my heart?"

Personal REFLECTION

1. Imagine that you are one of the disciples who listened to Jesus as He asked the question, "Who do you say that I am?" (Matthew 16:15). What will be your response?

2. At some point, most of us must confront the question of who will play the lead role and who will play the supporting role in our lives. At this moment, have you placed the Lord Jesus Christ into the leading role? If not, why not?

3. In the early Church, certain Christians lined up behind their favorite personalities so that Jesus' Lordship became lost in the mix. Is this a danger for you? If so, how do you overcome it?

4. Too many people confuse religion with relationship. How do you differentiate between the two?

5. Jesus' challenge to "deny yourself and take up your cross" seems like such a big assignment. What does that mean for you?

Personal PRAYER

Heavenly Father, I acknowledge that You sent Your Son, Jesus Christ, to be the real Rock Star of the Church. I also acknowledge that the Church belongs to Him, and that He will build it. Right now, I profess that He is the Christ, the Son of the living God, in my life. I place Him in the leading role and not the supporting role. I commit myself to a relationship with Him instead of religion. I intend to continue to deny myself, to take up my cross and to follow Him. I declare that I will not allow anyone or anything to take His place on the throne of my heart. Because I have heard His call to value godly character, I never want to exchange my soul for lesser priorities. I pray this in Jesus' name, Amen.

Group CHALLENGE

When Jesus asked His disciples the question, "Who do you say that I am?" (Matthew 16:15), He addressed the most important question of all time—"Who is Jesus?" In order to close the distance between us and God we must remain centered on this question. God will continue to interrupt our lives until we answer it in truth.

Sadly, the Church in the 21st century continues to struggle with the problem of the first-century Church—Christians lining up behind their favorite personality in place of Jesus Christ. To cultivate a rock star culture within the church remains diametrically opposed to the heart of God. Allow Peter's profession, "You are the Christ, the Son of the living God" (Matthew 16:16) to initiate group discussion about the identity of the real Rock Star of the Church—Jesus Christ.

1. Imagine that you are one of the disciples listening to Jesus ask the question, "Who do you say that I am?" What would your response be and why?

2. At some point, most of us confront the challenge of who will play the leading role and who will play the supporting role in our lives. Where would you say you are *right now* in that process?

3. In the early Church, certain Christians were lining up behind their favorite personalities, which allowed Christ Himself to get lost in the mix. How is this a danger in the Church today and how do we overcome it?

4. Too many people confuse religion with relationship. What is the difference for you?

5. Discuss the meaning of the following:

   a. denying yourself

   b. taking up your cross

   c. following Him

6. Sadly, everyone is confronted with temptations to lose or exchange their soul for some reward. What would some of those temptations be for you?

7. Discuss the call to character expressed by the apostle Paul: "My little children, for whom I labor in birth again until Christ is formed in you" (Galatians 4:19).

4

Download the God App

"You shall receive power when the Holy Spirit has come upon you; and you shall be witnesses to Me in Jerusalem, and in all Judea and Samaria, and to the end of the earth."

Acts 1:8

We live in an "intelligence age" that is driven by smart technology. Our phones have been smart for years, and now we also have smart homes, smart cars and even smart toys. Walk through a heavily populated area and you will see people focused on their screens—phone screens, tablet screens, laptop screens or television screens. Some people even like to look at multiple screens at the same time, and our kids can definitely be identified as "screenagers."

Of course, a couple of decades ago we did not have Instagram, iMessage, YouTube or Uber, and apps were unheard of. The Apple App Store distributed its first five hundred apps in July of 2008.[1] Now, we can choose from as many as 2.8 million apps on the Google Play store, and each day the average smartphone user spends an average of two hours and fifteen minutes on sixty to ninety apps downloaded on his or her phone.[2]

My daughter, Grace, downloads mostly gaming and social media apps, but on my phone I have all kinds of eatery apps—Chick-fil-A, Chili's and Starbucks, to name a few. I have an Andy's Frozen Custard app, which is not only my favorite app, but the all-time favorite of my whole family (maybe not so much because of the app itself as because of the delicious frozen custard it enables us to purchase). I also have transportation apps for Uber and American Airlines. I know that if my flight is delayed or canceled, I can book another flight on my phone in a matter of minutes. These invaluable apps help me get from one place to the next as conveniently as possible.

All of these apps have been made available by the software industry through "the cloud." And while cloud computing technically refers to storing and processing data via various online servers, for most people "the cloud" seems to mean something more like a sort of mystical or metaphysical realm. In consideration of all this, what if God has offered a sort of spiritual app that can connect earth to heaven at any time—an access point to His spiritual servers?

In actual fact, He has. The "God App" is always available to believers. It does not require a 5G network, rigorous safety precautions or the nebulous "cloud." Instead, God has established a direct link with us by means of His presence—the Holy Spirit. I am suggesting that the Holy Spirit is in effect our God App. In fact, by using the acronym APP we can remember that, through the Holy Spirit, we can . . .

Access the Presence of God's Power.

Right before He ascended to heaven, Jesus promised His disciples: "You shall receive power when the Holy Spirit has come upon you; and you shall be witnesses to Me in Jerusalem, and in all Judea and Samaria, and to the end of the earth" (Acts 1:8). In other words, they would "Access the Presence of His Power."

Access

To initiate access you must have decisive engagement. To gain access to my laptop, I must open it and provide the necessary password, which then admits me to the wealth of information stored there. In order to gain access to my house, I just use the right keys, without which I am locked out.

That reminds me of what happened after my family moved to Fort Worth, Texas, in 2017. To help ease the pain of the move and to create a measure of happy anticipation for this new chapter in her life, we promised our daughter, Grace, that we would get her a puppy. Eventually, after the first few months of setting up our new home, we bought her the promised puppy— a gorgeous brown-and-white-spotted Australian shepherd that we named Teddy. We were all enamored with this beautiful puppy, but of course we were not so thrilled about his potty training.

One night, Grace took Teddy out for his potty-training routine after midnight, and she accidently locked herself out of the house. She could not get back in because we had not yet put a spare key outside, and Mom and Dad were already sound asleep upstairs with their smartphones on mute (which certainly was not very smart). Without any solution in sight, Grace ended up sleeping in a lounge chair outside, hugging her puppy, even though the temperature dropped significantly that night. We can laugh about it now, but it was a bit traumatic at the time for Grace to be locked out of the house in the cold.

Have you ever been locked out of something? Locked out of your laptop, your car or even your house? When you are locked out, you can become distraught because you know you have a legal right of occupation while at the same time you experience a temporary loss of access.

I am here to remind you that the God App keeps us from experiencing any kind of spiritual lockout. This is because the God App was permanently installed in you when you first became a Christian. The apostle Paul explained:

> Don't you realize that your body is the temple of the Holy Spirit, who lives in you and was given to you by God? You do not belong to yourself, for God bought you with a high price. So you must honor God with your body.
>
> 1 Corinthians 6:19–20 NLT

At all times, we have divine access to God through the Holy Spirit. This is how the distance closes between us and God, as we are provided with two distinct benefits—the Holy Spirit helps us to lock out fleshly lusts, and He helps us to step free of the law. Let me explain. . . .

Lock Out the Lust of the Flesh

Recently, I was talking to a friend about the Holy Spirit. She had grown up in church from early in her life, and yet she still had many questions. "What does a 21st-century Spirit-led Christian look like? What does it really mean to access the life of the Spirit?" The apostle Paul addresses this question in his letter to the church in Galatia, when he wrote:

> I say then: Walk in the Spirit, and you shall not fulfill the lust of the flesh. For the flesh lusts against the Spirit, and the Spirit against the flesh; and these are contrary to one another, so that you do not do the things that you wish. But if you are led by the Spirit, you are not under the law.
>
> Galatians 5:16–18

When we access the life of the Spirit, the lust of the flesh is essentially locked out; no longer does sin have legal occupancy. The word *walk* (*paripateo* in Greek) actually paints the picture of "strolling in a familiar place." Have you ever used a walking or running path so often that you no longer have to think about where you are going? I have developed that kind of circular path around my neighborhood that is about a mile long. When I run while listening to a podcast or some well-chosen music, I do not even think about where I am going.

In much the same way, the Holy Spirit becomes part of your life constantly, just like breathing in and breathing out. He is always guiding and directing you in the life of the Spirit. No wonder the Scripture says, "In Him we live and move and have our being" (Acts 17:28). The Spirit-life remains familiar.

Of course, even as you grow familiar with the Spirit-life, a battle rages between the life of the Spirit and the lust of your flesh. The New Living Translation provides a more detailed picture:

> So I say, let the Holy Spirit guide your lives. Then you won't be doing what your sinful nature craves. The sinful nature wants to do evil, which is just the opposite of what the Spirit wants. And the Spirit gives us desires that are the opposite of what the sinful nature desires. These two forces are constantly fighting each other, so you are not free to carry out your good intentions. But

when you are directed by the Spirit, you are not under obligation to the law of Moses.

Galatians 5:16–18 NLT

Regrettably, a kind of "syrupy syncretism" or "sloppy agape" has emerged in some Christian circles today, and it has caused some people to minimize their spiritual nature and elevate the sin that remains alive within them. They make statements like this: "Because of my carnal nature, I just can't help but sin." Sometimes they will even emphasize Scriptures (or portions of Scriptures) to prove their point: "I'm just a sinner saved by grace, and I fall short of the glory of God." Or "If we say that we have no sin, we deceive ourselves, and the truth is not in us" (1 John 1:8).

Certainly, all of us are capable of sin because we do have a sinful nature that makes it quite possible at any time for us to sin. Yes, we are capable of sinning, but we do not have to continue to live in sin. The apostle Paul said, "Shall we continue in sin that grace may abound? Certainly not!" (Romans 6:1–2). As followers of Christ, we should be working diligently—with the ever-present help of the Holy Spirit—to avoid sin at all costs.

Actually, John the Beloved amplified his remarks (from 1 John 1:8) by declaring: "Whoever abides in Him does not sin. Whoever sins has neither seen Him nor known Him" (1 John 3:6). In both references to sin, the tense of the Greek verb indicates continuous action. The fact is, one who abides in Christ will not go on continually or habitually sinning as a way of life. In other words, John wrote: "Whoever has been born of God does not [continue to] sin, for His [God's] seed remains in him; and he cannot [continue to] sin, because he has been born of God" (1 John 3:9).

Christians cannot keep on sinning because God's seed remains inside them. It is interesting to note that the word *seed* here is the Greek word *sperma*. Sound familiar? Here John refers to a miraculous encounter—a spiritual miracle! When each one of us receives the gift of salvation, God's divine seed or *sperma* is deposited into our lives, and it carries the nature of God. It is a spiritual deposit. As a result, our desires begin to change, and we will never be the same again. Words and actions that did not seem to bother us previously now strike against our conscience. A greater sensitivity occurs in daily life because God's spiritual seed has been deposited in us.

Regardless of the nature of the seed—plant, animal or human—all seed produces after its kind. Apples produce apples. Dogs produce dogs. Humans produce humans. When we receive Jesus Christ as our Lord and Savior, God's seed begins to reproduce God in us. The nature of the seed of God produces the character of God in the person in whom it has been planted. And just as the seed develops into maturity and begins to produce fruit, so too does the seed of the Spirit begin producing the fruit of the Spirit (see Galatians 5:22–23). Over time, this spiritual fruit becomes more prevalent in us than the works of the flesh, which would have actually disqualified us from inheriting the Kingdom of God:

> Now the works of the flesh are evident, which are: adultery, fornication, uncleanness, lewdness, idolatry, sorcery, hatred, contentions, jealousies, outbursts of wrath, selfish ambitions, dissensions, heresies, envy, murders, drunkenness, revelries, and the like; of which I tell you beforehand, just as I also told you in time past, that those who practice [Greek *prasso*: keep on practicing] such things will not inherit the kingdom of God.
>
> Galatians 5:19–21

To access the life of the Spirit means that we begin to lock out the lust of the flesh not only temporarily, but permanently. Once again, God's seed (the Holy Spirit) enables us to walk in the Spirit. To the person who says, "I'm just a sinner saved by grace," the response becomes, "You *were* a sinner saved by grace, but now you are living the Spirit-life." To the one who says, "I fall short of the glory of God," the reminder becomes, "You fell short of the glory of God only until you received His God-seed in you."

Thankfully, because we all have access to the life of the Spirit, we no longer must fulfill the lust of the flesh.

Leave the Law of Moses Behind

When we gain divine access to God through the Spirit, we are enabled to leave the Law of Moses behind—the second distinct benefit: "But if you are led by the Spirit, you are not under the law" (Galatians 5:18). The meaning of "the law" is not confined only to the Old Testament Law. Obviously, there are certain commands in the Mosaic Law that are morally, ethically and spiritually timeless—the Ten Commandments, for example. But many Christians today ignore the traditional Jewish understanding of certain commandments such as "Remember the Sabbath day and keep it holy." Only a small number of Christians keep the Sabbath on Saturday and rarely does their observance involve the avoidance of all work—or use of electronics—as is Jewish custom.

The Old Testament Law is comprised of much more than just the Ten Commandments. In fact, there are 613 different laws described by Moses, many of which are difficult to apply to our current culture, such as, "You must not cook a young goat in its mother's milk" (Exodus 34:26 NLT), or "Do not wear clothing woven from two different kinds of thread" (Leviticus 19:19 NLT). And then there is this one: "And you may not eat the pig. It has split hooves but does not chew the cud, so it is ceremonially unclean for you" (Deuteronomy 14:8 NLT). There goes your breakfast bacon! Actually, some of Moses' laws might be helpful to follow in today's entitlement society, such as, "Stand up in the presence of the elderly, and show respect for the aged" (Leviticus 19:32 NLT).

When you read these examples, you might wonder, "Why do we adhere to some of Moses' laws while we ignore others?" This was a bigger quandary in the first-century Church, when the apostle Paul offered his thought: "But if you are led by the Spirit, you are not under the law." He had already clarified this earlier in his letter to the Galatian church:

> Before the way of faith in Christ was available to us, we were placed under guard by the law. We were kept in protective custody, so to speak, until the way of faith was revealed. Let me put it another way. The law was our guardian until Christ came; it protected us until we could be made right with God through faith. And now that the way of faith has come, we no longer need the law as our guardian. For you are all children of God through faith in Christ Jesus.
>
> Galatians 3:23–26 NLT

Now, please do not misunderstand me. I am not suggesting that Moses' laws are no longer present with us because they are. After all, Jesus expressed that He did not come to destroy them but to fulfill them (see Matthew 5:17). When He came, the standard changed from the Mosaic Law to His holiness.

To illustrate my point, think of an umbrella, that blessed apparatus that protects us from the rain. In the Old Testament, the umbrella was the Law, and it protected those who lived by it from sin. But now, because of the coming of Christ Jesus, we no longer need to live under the umbrella of the Law, since His death on the cross protects us from sin. In fact, we might even say that we now stand under the shadow of the cross; for it is the cross that has become our umbrella, not the Law, and it is the cross that protects us from the rain/reign of sin.

But again, His fulfillment of the Law did not actually do away with the Law altogether. If anything, He took certain portions of the Law to a whole new level. In the Sermon on the Mount, Jesus preached:

> "*[The Law] says*, 'You must not commit adultery.' *But I say*, anyone who even looks at a woman with lust has already committed adultery with her in his heart."
>
> Matthew 5:27–28 NLT, emphasis added

> "*[The Law] says* the punishment must match the injury: 'An eye for an eye, and a tooth for a tooth.' *But I say*, do not resist an evil person! If someone slaps you on the right cheek, offer the other cheek also."
>
> Matthew 5:38–39 NLT, emphasis added

The Law also says that you should go a mile when someone asks, but Jesus says that you should go an extra mile (see Matthew 5:40–41). Jesus often strengthened the parts of the Law that were universal and timeless (such as "you shall not commit adultery" or "you shall not murder"), but the parts of the Law that were cultural (such as eating hotdogs or wearing a polyester-cotton blend shirt), He left for personal application. This is affirmed in the Galatian narrative:

> For in Christ Jesus neither *circumcision* [circumcision is not a timeless moral law but a cultural or civil law] *nor uncircumcision* avails anything, but faith working through love.
>
> Galatians 5:6

Perhaps today we could superimpose this: "For in Christ Jesus neither pork consumption nor pork abstention avails anything, but rather faith working through love." Decisions about what

64

we eat or what we wear or even our choice of which days to worship on are of lesser importance, as these are not universal and timeless moral laws. The difference becomes clear if you inject a universal or timeless moral law into this Scripture, because it just does not work: "For in Christ Jesus neither murder nor non-murder avails anything, but rather faith working through love."

When we try to decide what is or is not a timeless moral truth, the bottom line is simple: Our lives, regardless of cultural constructs and societal norms, should always be subordinate to the Spirit of God. We live under the superior protection of our Umbrella. This is how our access of the grace-life of Christ's Spirit leaves the Law of Moses behind.

The Presence

When we refer to the "presence of God," we point to the Person of the Holy Spirit. Even though some Christians tend to speak of the Holy Spirit as an "it," the Holy Spirit is not a thing to use but rather a Person to know. He is more than a force; He is a Friend.

What distinguishes a person from a thing? Someone might say "life," but even a plant or a tree has life. The difference between plants and trees and human beings is the *soul*—the mind, the will and the emotions. Much the same as us, the Holy Spirit has a mind (thoughts), will (desires) and emotions (feelings). Here is how we know He has a mind: "He [Jesus] who searches the hearts knows what the mind of the Spirit is, because He makes intercession for the saints according to the will of God" (Romans 8:27).

Since the Holy Spirit has a mind, what would His IQ be? Actually, He does not have one. The formula known as intelligence quotient measures reasoning ability, and His intelligence cannot be measured, because God's Spirit knows everything about everything. Just think: We as Christians have Someone living on the inside who knows everything about everything.

The Holy Spirit has a mind and a will. If you have ever prayed, "Lord, show me what You want me to do," you have acknowledged that He has certain desires, and you have invited the Holy Spirit to make those desires known to you, so that you can be what He wants you to be, do what He wants you to do and go where He wants you to go. This is how Paul and Silas were able to obey the Spirit: "Now when they had gone through Phrygia and the region of Galatia, *they were forbidden by the Holy Spirit* to preach the word in Asia" (Acts 16:6, emphasis added).

And because the Spirit of God has emotions, we are told, "Do not grieve the Holy Spirit of God, by whom you were sealed for the day of redemption" (Ephesians 4:30). What happens if you say something that offends another person? The person may withdraw because of hurt feelings. Something similar can occur with the Holy Spirit as a result of our words or actions. If we cause Him grief, He can withdraw from us, and we can lose intimacy with Him.

Our goal is to build relationship with Him, and one of the ways we can do this is to develop an appetite for Him.

Develop an Appetite for the Spirit

Whatever you love, you will pursue, right? If you love certain foods, you will pursue them. I believe that if there could be such a thing as the "spiritual gift of food," I would have it. I put certain foods on my calendar because I have developed such an appetite for them.

Starbucks appears on my calendar many mornings because I have acquired a taste for iced caramel macchiatos, upside down, with light caramel drizzle. When I visit Santa Clarita, California, I put a certain taco truck on my calendar because it serves the best chicken tacos I have ever eaten in my life. I was never the same again after I tasted my wife's lasagna for the first time; it seemed like my tongue wanted to beat my brains half to death just to get to it. Caramel macchiatos, chicken tacos, lasagna—those foods remain a consistent part of my schedule and my life.

So, here is the question: Do we put the Holy Spirit on our calendar in the same way? Do we have an appetite for God the Holy Spirit that matches our love for God the Father and God the Son? In order to access His presence (what I have termed downloading the God App), we must purposefully develop a taste for the Holy Spirit.

Develop Dependence upon the Spirit

Sometimes people can have the idea that they do not need God's presence. They think that they are somewhat powerful on their own, like the woodpecker that was pecking on a tree when lightning struck the tree and split it right down the middle. As the woodpecker was flying away, it turned back and said, "Look what I did!"[3] Unless we establish an ongoing partnership with the Holy Spirit, we will have a distorted picture of what we can truly accomplish, and our self-imposed limitations will keep us from experiencing God's presence in our lives.

Did you know that as a Christ-follower you can live with the sure knowledge that God is with you everywhere you go? You can reach a point in your relationship with God that you sense His presence all the time. At home, you can sit at your dinner table and sense that He is there with you. When you drive through your neighborhood, you can sense He is in the car with you. When you live dependent upon the Holy Spirit, you can quiet your heart at any moment, allowing His presence to flood your awareness.

Sorry to say, some people prefer to access Him as if He were only their transportation app. They reach out to Him to save them in a moment of crisis or merely when they do not know how to get from one place to the next. They open the app only when they feel they need Him rather than leaving their location services on continually (as if to say, "Holy Spirit, I need You at all times and can do nothing without You.")

Recently, someone asked me, "How are you able to serve as the presiding bishop of an entire denomination?" Truthfully, to serve as the primary leader of the Pentecostal Church of God in nearly seventy nations remains an overwhelming assignment. The question was a valid one, and the only response I could muster was, "I am completely dependent upon the Holy Spirit."

Many times before I share the Word in sermonic form, I will kneel and offer a prayer, along with those in attendance. The gesture is not a mere ritual without a reason; it is my way of accessing the presence of the Holy Spirit and submitting to His will at that moment of time.

Our physical bodies will survive weeks without food and days without water, but only minutes without air. In the same way, without the breath of the Holy Spirit, we will not survive. Only His presence will sustain and empower us.

Pray to Be Used by the Spirit

Finally, as we learn to access the presence of the Holy Spirit, we will pray to be used by Him. What would change over the next seven days if you would ask the Holy Spirit to use you? What would you begin to see more frequently in your life?

Because the Bible calls the Holy Spirit the Comforter, we know we would comfort people more fervently. As we are led by Him, His comfort would reign in our daily lives, and the level of tension in our sphere of influence would begin to diminish. As comforters, we would experience a lot more blessing than stressing.

We would also find ourselves better able to guide people toward the truth, because the Holy Spirit guides people into all truth (see John 16:13). Our voices, hands and feet would represent Jesus in human skin and introduce others to the truth of the Kingdom.

Occasionally I will teasingly tell my wife, Kimberly, that God's voice in our home sounds a lot like her voice. With a laugh, I will declare that when I get to heaven, I expect God's voice to sound a lot like hers, as well. Of course, I say that in jest, but it is true that the Holy Spirit loves to use our voices as a representation of God's voice here on earth to guide others toward the truth. We become the living, breathing expression of an invisible Kingdom to a visible world. We become like a light display or a fireworks show to the world.

God's Power

God's power is central, not ancillary, to the life of every Christian. Jesus Himself affirmed this to His disciples when He declared:

> "Behold, I send the Promise of My Father upon you; but tarry in the city of Jerusalem until you are endued with power from on high."
>
> Luke 24:49

> "But you shall receive power when the Holy Spirit has come upon you; and you shall be witnesses to Me in Jerusalem, and in all Judea and Samaria, and to the end of the earth."
>
> Acts 1:8

How God anointed Jesus of Nazareth with the Holy Spirit and with power, who went about doing good and healing all who were oppressed by the devil, for God was with Him.

Acts 10:38

Access God's Supernatural Power

Some people choose to believe that the supernatural power of God disappeared with the early Christians, but they are unable to explain the miracles that still occur in current times. In Brazil not long ago, a middle-aged man wept before me as he shared the story of how his 74-year-old mother was miraculously healed of late-stage breast cancer. The doctors could not explain how the X-rays had come back without even a sign of the cancer's existence. Now because of this miracle, he and his sixteen brothers and sisters have given their lives to Christ.

I myself have experienced God's power to heal. For nearly twenty years, I endured an uncomfortable rash on my hands and feet. I went to doctors and received all kinds of creams. Some burned and some soothed, but I was never healed. Finally, I decided that every morning as I took a shower, I would thank God for my healing. Within six weeks, this problem that had tormented me for two decades had dried up and left my body. Stories such as these cannot be dismissed.

Oftentimes, when I say I am a Pentecostal Christian, people look puzzled or categorize me as one of those fanatical tongue-talkers, but that is not really what Pentecostalism means. Living as a Pentecostal Christian means that I believe that Jesus still does the same things today as He did when He walked the earth. In the 21st century, He still saves, heals, delivers, empowers and calls people, just as He did in the first century.

On the Day of Pentecost (see Acts 2), God presented a whole new way of living to Christ-followers—He placed the power of the Holy Spirit at the very center of the Church's faith and practice. The proclamation of the Gospel was confirmed through signs and wonders, and the Church was birthed as a supernatural people rather than ordinary people.

Unfortunately, mere talk about supernatural things will not change the world. The only way the world can be changed is by the supernatural lifestyles of the people of God. In other words, a superficial, talk-only gospel will be powerless; true reform and new life come only through a supernatural Gospel.

In general, it is true that some people pursue the presence of the Holy Spirit only because they want access to His power. But the truth is that God does not display His power to put on a show but only exclusively to make His Kingdom grow. His power will not be made available to "put on a shelf" but to overcome self. We can access God's powerful presence when we are committed to doing damage to the kingdom of darkness, taking Jesus' words seriously:

> "These miraculous signs will accompany those who believe: They will cast out demons in my name, and they will speak in new languages. They will be able to handle snakes with safety, and if they drink anything poisonous, it won't hurt them. They will be able to place their hands on the sick, and they will be healed."
>
> Mark 16:17–18 NLT

"These miraculous signs will accompany those who *believe*." Belief is the key. We fail to access God's power effectively because we do not believe that we can see the same things happen in the 21st century as in the first century. Because we have lacked signs and wonders, especially in the Western world, we have lacked evidence of God's power. Still, the greater danger for Christianity today is not necessarily *dismissing* the power of

Pentecost through unbelief but instead *accessing* the power of Pentecost carelessly. Imagine what would happen if we only believed!

Access God's Power to Witness

I traveled to New Orleans, Louisiana, in 2018 to attend a series of meetings with the Pentecostal Charismatic Churches of North America (PCCNA), a Christian organization devoted to collaboration among various Spirit-filled denominations. The largest Pentecostal and charismatic denominations in the world were represented at this meeting, and each organization, regardless of its size, brought a young leader in his or her twenties as a representative.

At the time, approximately twenty young leaders were present for a discussion forum and were asked the question: "What frustrates you the most where the Church is concerned?" Their answer was profound and poignant: "We are frustrated by Pentecostal leaders who preach about Pentecostal power but do not model it. They preach about signs and wonders, but they do not see them in action. They preach about winning the lost, but they do not win anyone themselves and certainly do not bring them to the church." They asked, "Why do our leaders not win anyone to the Lord and connect them to the Kingdom?" I was so deeply moved by what they shared that it took several weeks for me to process their response.

Throughout the twentieth century, the Pentecostal movement called itself a Full-Gospel or Five-Fold Gospel movement. The idea was that their methodology would encompass these five aspects: salvation, sanctification, the empowerment of the Holy Spirit, divine healing and the Second Coming of Christ. Unfortunately, many Pentecostals today have wavered, and Christians at large now tend to retreat into the shadows underneath their steeples because they have not introduced anyone to Christ since Noah was on the ark. They may use a spiritual language, but they do not live in Pentecostal power.

The true, genuine, authentic power of the first-century Church was not given so that people would join together, speak in tongues in a worship gathering and feel good about it; it was given to win the lost, expand the Kingdom and turn the world upside down. Is it possible that we have too many Christians who hype the *emotions* of Pentecost but who do not live the *expressions* of Pentecost? How many emphasize speaking in tongues while failing to share their faith?

If we hope to be endued with greater power again, we must do more than simply celebrate a Sunday worship experience. We must start to testify in the marketplace throughout the week. We must begin to offer a full Gospel to an empty world.

We know that the Bible teaches us to receive His power to witness. Therefore . . .

- Why would we keep talking about the things Jesus did in the first century without walking in the things Jesus is doing in the 21st century?
- Why would we claim that we are following the Great Commandment—seeking to love God and our neighbors as we love ourselves (see Matthew 22:36–39)—while we do not even know the names of our neighbors?
- Why would we want to preach three thousand sermons to win one person to Christ rather than one sermon to win three thousand?
- Why would we want to talk about the presence and power of the Holy Spirit if we do not live in the presence and power of the Holy Spirit?

Ultimately, we should not want to access His presence and His power in order to gain a special experience but always to accelerate the missional pace of the Kingdom.

Access God's Power to Communicate

When we access God's power our ability to communicate with God and others will grow. The Bible is clear about the fact that when people speak in tongues or a spiritual language, it is not mere "babbling speech" that they conjure up in their minds. They are not in some kind of hypnotic trance, muttering weird gibberish or a voodoo-like mumbo-jumbo. Spiritual language is a God-idea, not a man-idea, a heavenly plan and not a human plot, a divine blessing and not a demonic blight!

Scripture clarifies the difference between speaking in known languages and unknown languages:

> When the day of Pentecost had fully come, they were all with one accord in one place. . . . And they were all filled with the Holy Spirit and began to speak with other tongues, as the Spirit gave them utterance.
>
> Acts 2:1–4

Because these events occurred during a Jewish festival week in which people from all over the known world were present, the fact that they could hear people speaking in their own languages (and they recognized that the speakers could not have learned any of the languages) was an inspiring testimony to the power of the Holy Spirit to communicate God's message. God used it to birth the Church. The Spirit helped Peter explain to the crowd what was happening, and three thousand people came to faith in Christ that day (see Acts 2:14–41).

I can tell you from firsthand experience that God still allows people to speak in known languages miraculously. During one of my trips to Manaus, Brazil, I prayed for people at the end of the worship gathering at length and in tongues. Afterward, a young woman sent me a Facebook message, "Do you know Portuguese?" (Portuguese is the official language of Brazil.) Of course I do not know Portuguese, as evidenced by the fact that I had needed an interpreter in order to preach the message that night. She continued, "When you prayed over me, you shared that God was getting ready to open a door for me in Chile, and that I was to say yes and walk through that door." I had prayed over her in what I had perceived was an unknown language, yet God had used me to speak in a known language to direct this woman's life.

Occasionally, God uses speaking in tongues with known languages to communicate with people and to bring about His purposes, but more often God uses speaking in tongues with unknown languages to communicate with Him alone. We see examples of this in the New Testament. Look what happened on these two separate occasions with Peter and Paul:

> While Peter was still speaking these words, the Holy Spirit fell upon all those who heard the word. And those of the circumcision who believed were astonished, as many as came with Peter, because the gift of the Holy Spirit had been poured out on the Gentiles also. For they heard them speak with tongues and magnify God.
>
> Acts 10:44–46

> Then Paul said, "John indeed baptized with a baptism of repentance, saying to the people that they should believe on Him who would come after him, that is, on Christ Jesus." When they heard *this*, they were baptized in the name of the Lord Jesus. And when Paul had laid hands on them, the Holy Spirit came upon them, and they spoke with tongues and prophesied.
>
> Acts 19:4–6

Neither of these passages refers to "other tongues" or known languages, as was the case in Acts 2, because in those situations the Gentiles did not need to speak in a known language for others from around the world to hear and understand. Instead, they are speaking in a different kind of language, which Paul describes as follows:

> For he who speaks in a tongue does not speak to men but to God, for no one understands him; however, in the spirit he speaks mysteries.
>
> 1 Corinthians 14:2

> If you praise him in the private language of tongues, God understands you but no one else does, for you are sharing intimacies just between you and him.
>
> 1 Corinthians 14:2 Message

Neither the speaker nor the listener understands the language, but God does. This makes me think about a dear lady I met when I served as a pastor in Valencia, California. She was faithful in her church attendance even after she lost her ability to speak in 1996. She suffered from both apraxia and aphasia, which meant that she could no longer position her tongue or her lips to speak the words that should come out of her mouth. On many occasions, she would take my face in her hands and, with amazing love in her gaze, she would utter a number of guttural sounds. She knew exactly what she wanted to say or pray, but no longer could say it intelligibly. When I remember my experience with this dear woman, I am reminded of how often I have all kinds of thoughts and feelings that I cannot put into words; I simply do not know how to verbalize them. When I pray in an unknown language, however, I am able to communicate all my spiritual secrets directly to the heart of God.

Download the God App

When we download the God App, we access God's power for the supernatural, God's power to witness and God's power to communicate with Him and others. Yet the challenge remains: Will we choose to live by miracles or by mantras? With signs and wonders or with sayings? Our world needs more than motivational speeches and sermons about behavior modification; we need to access the presence of God's power.

When we consider the scriptural evidence, we can no longer overlook the connection between accessing the presence of God's power and speaking by the power of His Spirit in both known and unknown languages. The known languages communicate to others while the unknown languages communicate directly to God.

Our ability to engage the Spirit in our lives is not based on denominational affiliation. Instead, it is simply a matter of drawing nearer to God. You can be Catholic, Episcopal, Baptist or Presbyterian and still download the God App. It does not matter who you are or where you come from, God's presence is accessible to every believer. We too often forget this. The apostle Paul asks this question of the Galatian Christians: "Are you so foolish? Having begun in the Spirit, are you now being made perfect by the flesh?" (Galatians 3:3).

As Christ-followers, we did not begin in the Law; we began in the Spirit. The Law did not activate our lives; the Spirit did. How then can we draw nearer to God unless we search for the person of the Holy Spirit and engage with Him? We have been promised already that our search is guaranteed to yield fruitful results and that we will not come up short. Only after a search (something like spiritual internet browsing) will we find Him. Then all we need to do to access the presence of His power is to say yes with a virtual click on the words *Download the God App.*

Personal CHALLENGE

If you have developed a taste for lobster, shrimp cocktail or chocolate mousse, you will make an effort to obtain those foods. Where God is concerned, every one of us who has called on the name of Christ Jesus should develop an appetite and preference—a growing hunger and thirst—for the life of the Spirit. As we develop an appetite for the Spirit, He will find ways of connecting with us directly on a consistent basis.

In an interesting application of this concept, the apostle Paul said: "If we live in the Spirit, let us also walk in the Spirit" (Galatians 5:25). Why would Paul make a distinction between living in the Spirit and walking in the Spirit unless there is one? Why would he imply that there is something more if there is not? He does not want us to settle for what we may call "living in the Spirit" when we can simultaneously walk alongside God and experience a greater closeness with Him.

Your personal challenge will be to follow through and download the God App, by means of which you can "Access the Presence of God's Power" and lock out the enemy. This is God's personal promise to you: ". . . *when* the Holy Spirit has come upon you . . ." (Acts 1:8, emphasis added).

Personal REFLECTION

1. How would you compare the time you spend with your apps on your smartphone to your time with God?

2. Do you notice the struggle inside between the lust of the flesh and the life of the Spirit? How do you think it would help to access the presence of God's power?

3. How did this chapter's section "Leave the Law of Moses Behind" help your spiritual journey?

4. How are you developing an appetite for the Holy Spirit and praying to be used by Him?

5. What are your thoughts regarding your personal search for the Holy Spirit so that you can see more supernatural power, witness and communicate with God?

Personal PRAYER

Heavenly Father, I desperately need access to the presence of Your power. I need a personal relationship with the Person of the Holy Spirit. Right now, I call upon You and am aware that You are listening. Holy Spirit, come and empower me to be a tangible expression of Your invisible Kingdom. Enable me to access Your supernatural power, Your power to witness and Your power to communicate Your message in a more effective way. Help me to have the courage to reach out to You, to close the distance between You and me. Amen and amen.

Group CHALLENGE

The call to download the God App is a call to pursue the Holy Spirit. His continued partnership allows us to draw nearer to God. Allow this purposeful pursuit to initiate a group discussion.

1. Discuss your reflections about the comparison between the time spent on your smartphone with your time spent with God.

2. What are your thoughts about this statement?—"The Holy Spirit is a Person to know rather than a thing to use."

3. Discuss the following directives:

    a. Lock out the lust of the flesh, so that the Holy Spirit will win the war between the lust of the flesh and the life of the Spirit.

    b. Leave the Law behind, so that the Holy Spirit can offer us freedom to replace restrictive cultural laws.

4. How are you developing an appetite for the Holy Spirit, and how are you praying to be used by Him?

5. Discuss these four aspects of walking with the Spirit:

    a. Accessing God's power for the supernatural

    b. Accessing God's power to witness

    c. Accessing God's power to communicate with God

    d. Accessing God's power to "walk in the Spirit."

5

Mind the Gaptivity

"If My people who are called by My name will humble themselves, and pray and seek My face, and turn from their wicked ways, then I will hear from heaven, and will forgive their sin and heal their land."

2 Chronicles 7:14

No sooner had King Solomon said amen in his prayer of dedication for the newly constructed temple than a shaft of fire plummeted earthward and filled the place with a burst of glory. What a flashy entrance for God—a true divine interruption! I wish I could have been there as an observer to see the reactions of the priests as they froze right in their glory-tracks, unable to enter the building. The whole congregation was forced to hit the deck, foreheads to the pavement, in the presence of the divine glory-fire.

As far as celebrations go, this was a national extravaganza. And although we cannot be sure of its viewer rating, we know that it was a 22,000-cattle-and-120,000-sheep kind of event, most likely the biggest one in the national history of Israel. The party lasted for two weeks. Finally, when it began to disperse, God appeared to King Solomon, and He pointed to the fine print of His new housing arrangement. As the new tenant in His temple, God wanted to ensure that His people understood the contract. His declaration went something like this:

> "I have heard your prayer, and have chosen this place for Myself as a house of sacrifice."
>
> 2 Chronicles 7:12

So far, so good.

> "When I shut up heaven and there is no rain, or command the locusts to devour the land, or send pestilence among My people . . ."
>
> 2 Chronicles 7:13

So far, not so good.

Can you imagine Solomon's thoughts at that moment? "God, we just spent two weeks cheering You on while You moved into Your house. Now You warn us about upcoming drought and pestilence. Why would You allow that?" Undoubtedly, it was because the sovereign God wanted to make sure that Solomon knew He was absolutely supreme. The almighty God wanted to acquaint Solomon with the power of divine interruption. He showed what happens when His people do not "mind the gap" where their spiritual distance from Him is concerned.

The phrase "Mind the gap" was coined by the London Underground in the late sixties when they automated their subway system. It is now used for transit systems worldwide to remind passengers that a potentially unsafe spatial gap exists between the train and station platform.[1] I took the idea of minding the gap and combined it with the word *activity* to form a new term: *gaptivity*. Gaptivity refers to the spiritual gap or distance that can develop between us and God even after we have experienced tangible expressions of His presence, a gap that we fill with an overload of daily activities. How often can the warp speed of our active lives warp our souls?

As Christians, we can even try to close the distance between ourselves and God by attempting to succeed in life despite the fact that our souls are disconnected from Him. All too easily, we can interpret our successes and victories as indications of God's presence and blessing. When we with God's people have just enjoyed a 22,000-cattle-and-120,000-sheep event, or when God's glory has been revealed in the church house, it is easy to declare, "God is great and God is good; let us thank Him for our food." But when we start to experience drought, devastation and disease, we come up against soul warfare. The splattered grasshoppers on our spiritual windshield remind us that the dust is blowing, the locusts are thriving and folks are dying. Where is God then?

Even though the temple dedication was a rousing success, God was beginning to prepare Solomon and His people to "mind the gaptivity." He issued a challenge that presented an "if-then" relationship with Him:

> "*If* My people who are called by My name will humble themselves, and pray and seek My face, and turn from their wicked ways, *then* I will hear from heaven, and will forgive their sin and heal their land."
>
> 2 Chronicles 7:14, emphasis added

To close the distance between ourselves and God, we must enter into a sacred cooperation with Him. The initial interruption belongs to Him while the response belongs to us. When He interrupts our lives and invites us into a personal partnership, He provides conditions, challenges and consequences to help us succeed.

In this instance, the guidelines were quite clear:

The *condition*: "If My people, who are called by My name . . ."

The *challenge*: ". . . Will humble themselves and pray and seek my face and turn from their wicked ways . . ."

The *consequence*: ". . . Then I will hear from heaven and will forgive their sin and heal their land."

The Condition

("If My people, who are called by My name . . .") God prefaces the benefits of relationship with Him by making it clear that we must identify with His family and name. We must declare that we rightfully belong to Him, which means that we acknowledge His sovereignty, finding our home in His care.

My own two sons and daughter are known as "my" children because my wife and I have taken ownership and responsibility for them. They recognize that wherever Mom and Dad are located, they are home. At home, they have access to the resources that meet every identifiable need. When they are hungry and thirsty, they do not expect anyone else to buy them groceries; Mom and Dad will provide. If they need a pair of shoes, they will not look to someone else to purchase them because Mom and Dad will always do it. They are at home with us, and my wife and I take full responsibility for them.

In much the same way, when we identify as part of God's family (God's people), our Father God takes ownership and responsibility for us. He remains intentionally committed to our care. "And my God shall supply all your need according to His riches in glory by Christ Jesus" (Philippians 4:19). He becomes our sovereign Father, and we are always at home in Him.

And as a part of His family, we bear His name. In the Old Testament, the name of God was unspeakable. It was considered to be so holy that rabbis and priests would commonly refer to God as Adonai, which means "My Lord," and when they needed to write His name, they almost always left out its vowels. The ancient scrolls refer to God as Y-H-W-H. In their effort to keep God's official name sacred, the Hebrews developed many names for Him over time, for example "Hashem," which literally means "the Name."

But in the New Testament, a new name was introduced to God's people. The apostle Paul records this:

> And being found in appearance as a man, He [Jesus] humbled Himself and became obedient to the point of death, even the death of the cross. Therefore God also has highly exalted Him and given Him the name which is above every name, that at the name of Jesus every knee should bow, of those in heaven, and of those on earth, and of those under the earth, and that every tongue should confess that Jesus Christ is Lord, to the glory of God the Father.
>
> Philippians 2:8–11

When Jesus, the Christ, appeared to humankind, a name was introduced that changed the course of human history. And when He was exalted to heaven, that name was given its rightful authority above every name. "Now he is far above any ruler or authority or power or leader or anything else—not only in this world but also in the world to come" (Ephesians 1:21 NLT). In the words of the familiar hymn, "All hail the power of Jesus' name! Let angels prostrate fall; bring forth the royal diadem and crown Him Lord of all."

When we declare that we are part of God's people, we acknowledge His sovereignty—His place as King. And when we accept His sacred name, Jesus Christ, we also acknowledge His authority—His power as Lord. Because of this, we, like little children, can dwell in complete peace, confident that we are at home with Him.

The Challenge

(". . . Will humble themselves and pray and seek my face and turn from their wicked ways . . .") The key words here are "humility," "hunger" and "holiness," and they sum up God's challenge to us as His sons and daughters. Allow me to explain what I mean.

Personally, I love challenges. If you want to motivate me, just tell me that I cannot do something. When I first entered college as a freshman, one of my music professors told me that I could not sing well enough to select vocal music as an academic concentration. I took his declaration as a challenge, and I did it anyway. As it turned out, I graduated with the highest honors offered by the music department. Before the graduation ceremony, that same professor acknowledged that I had performed one of the best vocal recitals in the history of the college up to that point.

Of course, positive results are not guaranteed when we take up a challenge. On the positive side, challenges cause us to set goals and work hard to achieve them. But on the other hand, challenges can coerce us into accomplishing those goals for the wrong reasons.

Here, God's challenge to His people sets forth a threefold goal of *humility* ("if My people will humble themselves"), *hunger* ("and seek my face") and *holiness* ("and turn from their wicked ways").

Humility

One of the greatest scriptural principles for minding the gaptivity remains this one: "God opposes the proud but gives grace to the humble" (James 4:6 NLT). The proud and arrogant may achieve success through their own efforts, but they will only widen the gap between themselves and God because He opposes them.

God wants us to be dependent upon Him. God-dependence involves more than an acknowledgment of our absolute reliance upon Him; it involves a constant pursuit. On a daily basis, we must look to Him for divine strength and, with His help, appropriate it.

The very first Bible verse I memorized as a child was, "I can do all things through Christ who strengthens me" (Philippians 4:13). My parents, who were pastors at the time, would stand me up on the piano bench during the worship service and ask me to share Philippians 4:13. Even though as a four-year-old I did not understand the full extent of what I was sharing, I knew that Christ was somehow my Helper at that moment.

When we become God-dependent, we acknowledge on a daily basis that God empowers us to do things greater than we can do on our own. Actually, self-forgetfulness is a primary characteristic of God-dependence. When we forget about ourselves, God is exalted and we are not, which is the greatest testimony of all. We end up operating with the mindset that without God we are only one stitch away from unraveling, one step away from falling off a cliff or one breath away from drowning.

One day I took my son Garrett to lunch, and we had a good conversation about humility. I told him that humble people do not need to exalt themselves, because God does, usually through other people. I encouraged him to refrain from talking about his accomplishments in favor of allowing God and others to boast about them. The Scripture declares: "Humble yourselves in the sight of the Lord, and He will lift you up" (James 4:10). Garrett "got it." From that day forward, he began to acknowledge that humble people do not need to share about their accomplishments because God will make them known. He had learned that sometimes the greatest step that we can take toward God is to remember what He has done and forget what we have done.

Hunger

We must cultivate the spiritual hunger that causes us to seek His face. Recently, my wife and I watched a movie, *War Room*, which illustrated this principle. The movie presents a narrative about a grandma who taught a young Christian woman how to turn her wardrobe closet into a war room of prayer. As the young woman pursued this challenge throughout the movie, she began to close the distance between herself and God, and along the way her lackluster marriage was restored.

If we pay attention, we will learn from personal experience that our hunger for Him leads to prayer—which leads to more hunger for Him. A LifeWay study on pastoral prayer revealed that the more time pastors spend in prayer, the more satisfied they are with their relationship with God. Those who spent about an hour in prayer each day were very satisfied while those who spent twenty minutes or less were very dissatisfied.[2] Even though this study focused on pastors, I expect that the results would look the same if they were applied to any Christ-follower.

The implication of these results is not necessarily that Christ-followers must spend an hour or any other specific amount of time in prayer each day, but rather that the effort they put into seeking God makes all the difference. Quite simply, the people who spend more time in prayer each day have a more satisfying relationship with God.

Pray

Our primary challenge with prayer usually involves consistency and sustainability. How do we engage *daily* in prayer? How do we treat prayer as a first response rather than a last resort? In short, how do we ensure that prayer becomes a daily discipline in our lives?

First, write God into your daily calendar. Just as you make an appointment with a colleague or friend, make an appointment with God. Find a time of day when you are the most likely to be able to be alone with Him, to hush your heart before Him: "Be still, and know that I am God" (Psalm 46:10).

When my kids were growing up, there were times when I thought they must have "ants in their pants"; it seemed like they could not sit still for even ten seconds. Most of us have developed good rhythms for daily life, but unfortunately, these patterns of activity can present an ants-in-the-pants problem for us when it comes to prayer.

John Ortberg once said, "A lifestyle of hurrying is not about a disordered schedule, but a disordered heart."[3] In other words, if we can order our hearts, we will be able to order our schedules. Prayer does not have to be overly complicated; we simply close the door on our busy schedules and quiet our hearts before Him.

Second, study the Bible, which is God's voice to every generation. Recognize that when you read God's Word, you will become more able to hear God's voice. When you take the time to interact with the Bible, you open your heart to hear God's voice in the daily decisions of your life.

Finally, write down your thoughts and impressions from God. This is often called journaling. Through the years I have gone back and reread my thoughts, and they have had an impact on me time and again. Journaling can be a wonderful and worthwhile part of your time in prayer.

Indeed, you may well find that when you start setting appointments with God for prayer, Bible study and journaling, you have a new problem—not having *enough* time with God. No longer will you have to cope with too much empty, distracted time; now you will feel that you do not have enough time with God.

Of course, not all of this time will feel restful and pleasant. Some of it will be spent doing battle in prayer. The apostle Paul reminded us that while we do not wrestle with enemies that are flesh and blood, we have been enlisted by God to combat the spiritual evil in this world:

> This is no afternoon athletic contest that we'll walk away from and forget about in a couple of hours. This is for keeps, a life-or-death fight to the finish against the Devil and all his angels.
>
> Ephesians 6:12 MESSAGE

Like a fierce sports competition, the end result can often come down to the issue of how much we want to win in prayer. Are you hungry for God? How devotedly do you seek Him? How strong is your passion for engaging the forces of heaven against the forces of hell? You and I are in a lifelong life-or-death struggle, and only our King can keep us on the victorious side. Therefore, we must hunger to pray and seek His face.

Seek His Face

When you make prayer a part of the consistent and sustainable rhythm of your life, you will naturally begin to seek His face. Your prayer and devotional time will transition from something that may have felt like a duty or an obligation toward something you desire and look forward to, a more intimate time of face-to-face interaction with God.

Psychologists have used the word *attunement* to describe a phenomenon that happens with babies.[4] At some point in a baby's early development, he or she will look up from the crib and notice a face looking back. The baby will recognize that someone is paying attention; a connection with another person gets established. When the baby smiles, the other face smiles back. Certain expressions elicit certain responses.

In the Old Testament, we read words about God the Father's blessing that sound similar to attunement, "The Lord bless you and keep you; the Lord make His face shine upon you and be gracious to you; the Lord lift up His countenance upon you, and give you peace" (Numbers 6:24–26). Each of us as God's children can be connected to—or in tune with—our Creator. When we look up, we experience Him looking back at us. When we seek His face, we can feel that His face shines upon us, creating an atmosphere of peace.

Paul made his own decision to seek God's face. Even when he was bound in chains and sequestered in a dark prison cell, he prayed fervently for an open door to preach the Word and expand the Church. From his prison cell in Rome, he wrote to the church in Colossae:

> Continue earnestly in prayer, being vigilant in it with thanksgiving; meanwhile praying also for us, that God would open to us a door for the word, to speak the mystery of Christ, for which I am also in chains, that I may make it manifest, as I ought to speak.
>
> Colossians 4:2–4

This was a call to fervent, vigilant prayer.

You and I may not be locked in prison cells, but we, too, can enter into fervent times of prayer against the powers of darkness to see the mystery of Christ preached and the Kingdom of God expanded around the globe.

Holiness

God's encouragement to us to "mind the gaptivity" extends also to the pursuit of holiness, so that those who pray and seek His face "will turn from their wicked ways" (2 Chronicles 7:14). Although many people view holiness through a predetermined list of "dos and don'ts" of the Christian faith, the authentic nature of holiness does not work that way. When we allow God to get close enough to deploy a "search and destroy mission" against all of our sinful ways, we will begin to grow in holiness. True holiness comes when you invite God to evaluate your heart: "Search me, O God, and know my heart; try me, and know my anxieties; and see if there is any wicked way in me, and lead me in the way everlasting" (Psalm 139:23–24).

We can attempt to hide from God, just like Adam and Eve, who first sinned in the Garden and then hid themselves in the bushes when He called out to them (see Genesis 3). How many of us hide from God and engage in spiritual distancing? Not many of us invite a closer inspection, do we? How many people will not attend a church gathering because they are afraid God will ask for entrance through the door of their heart? People who really desire to get close to God will come out from behind the bushes, acknowledge their nakedness and ask God to come close. They will not hide—they will *welcome* repentance.

Naturally, those who pull back when they hear the word *repentance* are usually the ones who need repentance the most. But those who are willing to pray, "Search me, O God, and know my heart . . . and see if there is any wicked way in me" open themselves to the "way everlasting." With God's presence in their lives, they will be enabled to root out those sinful ways of life that stand as barriers in their spiritual journey.

Fortunately, we do not need to worry about how to identify our wicked ways on our own, because God will reveal them to us. The repentance part remains with us while the revelation part remains with God. This is important: Repentance often precedes a divine interruption in our lives.

Prior to Christ's coming in the first century, "there was a man, sent from God, whose name was John" (John 1:6). John's message was one of repentance: "Repent, for the kingdom of heaven is at hand" (Matthew 3:2). John's ministry of repentance preceded God's divine interruption—the coming of the Lord. You could say that repentance in the form of John preceded revelation in the form of Christ.

Francis Frangipane once said, "Every season of significant spiritual growth in your walk with God will be precipitated by a time of deep repentance."[5] To see spiritual growth, we must welcome repentance.

Repentance initiates the process of turning from our wicked ways, but renunciation authenticates it. God does not seek for a superficial sign of repentance on the outside but a spiritual change on the inside. When repentance and renunciation converge, we move beyond the mere expression of sorrow for our sin, and we begin to develop a deep sensitivity for what it means to live a holy life before the Lord.

Renunciation "affirms the turn." If we repent from our wicked ways but fail to turn from them, we abort our repentance. When we do that, our repentance remains a superficial attempt at giving birth to spiritual growth, and our distance from God grows wider. But when we not only repent but also renounce our sin, God comes swiftly to help us change; we grow beyond forgiveness for our sins into true holiness.

The Consequence

("... Then I will hear from heaven and will forgive their sin and heal their land.")

If we meet God's initial condition (by accepting our identity as His people who are called by His name) and we accept His challenge (by humbling ourselves, seeking His face and turning from our wicked ways), then we will receive the blessed consequences from His hand: "... Then I will hear from heaven and will forgive their sin and heal their land" (2 Chronicles 7:14).

This is the modus operandi of God. He is an "if-then" God. After you get on board with an "if you will do this" statement, He reciprocates with "then I will bless you." Thus: "If you will humble yourselves and pray . . . then I will hear from heaven and act." When God's people accept a challenge from Him, they reap His reward.

"I will hear from heaven and forgive their sin"

At Solomon's Temple dedication, where God spoke the words we read in 2 Chronicles 7:14, God promised to hear from heaven. Does His promise in this instance mean that He does not hear at other times? Some people would say, "Of course God hears us at *all* times, because He is always with us." Yet God's hearing appears to be conditional in many cases. For example, Isaiah the prophet declared: "But your iniquities have separated you from your God; and your sins have hidden His face from you, *so that He will not hear*" (Isaiah 59:2, emphasis added).

According to Isaiah, God's hearing was muted by the iniquities and sins of His people. So when God challenges His people to "turn from their wicked ways," He calls them to unmute the volume so He can hear from heaven and forgive their sins.

Regrettably, no thanks to their religious leaders, some people have lost their hope in God's forgiveness. Their leaders have mowed them down with discouraging words that are like machine guns on a battlefield. Their words may have been meant to convict people of their sin, but instead, whether intentionally or unintentionally, they have only convinced people of their hopeless condition. In addition, to make matters worse, Satan, the enemy of all humankind, will attack even sincere Christians, whispering, "You claim to be a Christian, but look how you have sinned again. Enough is enough. This time your sin will not be forgiven." Satan knows that if he can cause Christians to doubt God's forgiveness, then he can destroy their relationship with God.

This is why God speaks up as He did with the people of Israel, when He declared:

> "Why didn't anyone answer when I called? Is it because I have no power to rescue? No, that is not the reason! For I can speak to the sea and make it dry up! I can turn rivers into deserts covered with dying fish."
>
> Isaiah 50:2 NLT

In other words, God asked His people, "Listen, do you think the enemy has chopped off My mighty arm? Do you not believe that I have the power to rescue you from any situation?" These are rhetorical questions, of course, because He is far from powerless. If we will only repent and renounce our sin, He promises to hear, forgive and heal our land.

"I will heal their land"

What does God mean when He says "I will heal their land"? We must come to understand what He means so that we can be quick to recognize the healing when it comes. This seems hard to grasp, and yet it is very important. It carries clear consequences.

When God declared that He would heal the nation of Israel after their exile into Babylon, He not only pointed to a parcel of ground but to the people themselves: "Behold, I will bring it [the land] health and healing; I will heal them [the people] and reveal to them the abundance of peace and truth" (Jeremiah 33:6). God certainly has a unique place in His heart for the holy land of Israel, but He also has a heart for His *people*. That is why, eventually, He sent His Son to heal His people.

Perhaps we can gain some insight through the message that Peter preached after the nation of Israel had rejected and crucified Jesus. On the Day of Pentecost, Peter boldly proclaimed:

> "Repent therefore and be converted, that your sins may be blotted out, so that times of refreshing may come from the presence of the Lord, and that He may send Jesus Christ, who was preached to you before, whom heaven must receive until the times of restoration of all things, which God has spoken by the mouth of all His holy prophets since the world began."
>
> Acts 3:19–21

Just as God called the people to repent in 2 Chronicles 7:14, Peter also called for repentance, but with an interesting twist: ". . . that times of refreshing may come from the presence of the Lord," in effect saying, "Because you crucified the Messiah, your sin created a sort of dam that blocked the massive, life-giving flood of God's presence."

Actually, the literal language of this passage is that of wind and not water because the Greek word *anapsuxis* represents the "recovery of breath."[6] Peter declared that healing would come through a wave of fresh air that would enable God's people to breathe again. Just as when a dead body comes back to life, the land and people would be revived by waves of God's breath.

We must not forget that Peter's message was preached on the Day of Pentecost immediately after the hundred and twenty disciples in the Upper Room in Jerusalem had experienced the fresh wind or breath of God:

> When the Day of Pentecost had fully come, they were all with one accord in one place. And suddenly there came a sound from heaven, as of a rushing mighty wind, and it filled the whole house where they were sitting.
>
> Acts 2:1–2

It was immediately after this Acts 2 encounter that Peter declared to the assembled crowd:

> "'In the last days,'" God says, "'I will pour out my Spirit upon all people. Your sons and daughters will prophesy. Your young men will see visions, and your old men will dream dreams. In those days I will pour out my Spirit even on my servants—men and women alike—and they will prophesy.'"
>
> Acts 2:17–18 NLT

The scriptural implication here is that when God heals the land, He also sends fresh waves of His breath or presence to revive the spiritually dead and renew the spiritually weak. As Peter declared, the refreshing breath of God's Spirit pours out onto all flesh. Unbelievers come to life in Christ. Believers experience renewed life in Christ.

Of course, just as God reminded Solomon after the temple dedication extravaganza, we as His people have a vital role to play. We must intentionally "mind the gaptivity" to ensure that "times of refreshing may come from the presence of the Lord." We must remember God's condition, God's challenge and God's consequence:

> The *condition*: "If My people, who are called by My name . . ."

The *challenge*: ". . . Will humble themselves and pray and seek my face and turn from their wicked ways . . ."

The *consequence*: ". . . Then I will hear from heaven and will forgive their sin and heal their land."

If we do our part, *then* God promises to do His.

Personal CHALLENGE

Unless you "mind the gaptivity" of your relationship with God, the rollercoaster of life just keeps going endlessly, and you cannot get off. You can never overcome the extremes as long as you hurl up and down and all around. But if you choose to "mind the gaptivity," here are God's promises:

If you are broken, He will fix you.

If you are confused, He will guide you.

If you are hurt, He will heal you.

If you are fearful, He will protect you.

If you are stressed, He will give you peace.

If you are separated from God, He will save you.

Personal REFLECTION

1. How would you evaluate the health of your soul and its connection with God at this time? Do you feel well-connected with God, or distant from Him?

2. In 2 Chronicles 7:14, God challenges His people to "mind the gaptivity" in several areas. Please evaluate yourself according to the following:

a. humility (God-dependence and self-forgetfulness)

b. prayer (personal prayer and seeking His face)

c. repentance (personal repentance and renunciation)

3. This quick survey will provide some direction for reflection concerning the state of your prayer life:

   a. Are you satisfied with your prayer life?

   b. Do you pray with confidence and boldness?

   c. When someone asks you to pray for a need, do you really do it?

   d. What are five prayer requests that you have brought to the Lord this week?

   e. Is your prayer time comparable in length to your Bible-reading time?

   If you answered yes on at least three of these questions, it shows that you are making some positive strides forward in prayer. If you answered yes on two questions or fewer, realize that you need to give some more focused time to prayer. (Yet if you answered yes on the first question, you definitely need to give immediate attention to your prayer life because no one should be completely satisfied with the state of his or her prayer life.)

   Do not be concerned as much with the ebb and flow of prayer as with the goal of establishing it as a priority and continuously seeking His face.

4. Some people have lost their hope in God's forgiveness. Evaluate your "hope level" regarding God's ability to forgive your sin.

5. Some people have lost their hope in God's willingness to heal our land. Evaluate your "hope level" in God's ability to heal our land.

Personal PRAYER

Heavenly Father, I am desperate to "mind the gaptivity." I boldly declare that nothing is impossible for You. Please increase the level of my spiritual intimacy with You. Help me to come out from hiding in the bushes, and help me overcome every barrier that stands between us. I want to see the large obstacles and even my wicked ways destroyed, so that I can experience times of refreshing in Your presence. In Jesus' name, Amen.

Group CHALLENGE

"Mind the gap" was a phrase coined by the London Underground in 1968 but is now used for transit systems worldwide to constantly remind passengers that a spatial gap exists between the train and station platform.[7] So, while the term *gaptivity* is not an official word, it introduces the combination of two words—gap and activity. Allow this idea to direct your group discussion.

1. How would you evaluate the health of your soul at this time? Do you feel well-connected with God, or distant from Him? Discuss.

2. Share about some of the different ways we can allow a spiritual gap to develop between ourselves and God even after we have experienced tangible expressions of His presence.

3. What does true humility look like? Discuss the difference between God-dependence and self-reliance.

4. God challenges His people to pray and seek His face. Discuss the difference between the two.

5. The following quick survey will provide some direction for reflection concerning the state of your prayer life. Share your personal evaluations with the group.

   a. Are you satisfied with your prayer life?

   b. Do you pray with confidence and boldness?

   c. When someone asks you to pray for a need, do you really do it?

   d. What are five prayer requests that you have brought to the Lord this week?

   e. Is your prayer time comparable in length to your Bible-reading time?

   If you answered yes on at least three of these questions, it shows that you are making some positive strides forward in prayer. If you answered yes on two questions or fewer, realize that you need to give some more focused time to prayer. (Yet if you answered yes on the first question, you definitely need to give immediate attention to your prayer life because no one should be completely satisfied with the state of his or her prayer life.)

   We should not be concerned as much with the ebb and flow of our prayer as we are with the establishment of prayer as a priority. It is all-important to seek His face continuously.

6. Some people have lost their hope in God's personal forgiveness. Discuss what you have discovered regarding your "hope level" in God's ability to forgive your sin.

7. Some people have lost their hope in God's willingness to heal our land. What is your "hope level" in God's ability to heal our land, and why do you feel this way?

6

Hear from Heaven

"If anyone has ears to hear, let him hear."

Mark 4:23

Just before his junior year in high school, my oldest son, Spencer, approached me with tears in his eyes saying, "Dad, can I talk to you?" Of course, all kinds of fireworks started exploding in my head as my often shy and reserved son would never have requested a private conversation with me unless it was an emergency. I thought to myself, "Oh no, I'm getting ready to hear something I don't want to hear."

During that particular summer, Spencer and I had investigated several colleges for possible attendance after his high school graduation. If anyone asked Spencer concerning the next step in his life, he would say, "I plan to play baseball in college." As a standout athlete in high school, he was hoping to explore college athletics, and with a 4.0 GPA, he was poised to play for any number of schools. So what could he want to talk about? As we walked to the master bedroom for our conversation, I kept praying under my breath, "Lord, *please* help me. If there has ever been a time I need to hear from heaven, it's right now."

After a few awkward moments, he started telling me about his experience at church camp a couple of weeks earlier. During one of the worship gatherings, where hundreds of young people were standing and worshiping the Lord, he shared what had happened to him. By this time, tears were flooding down his cheeks as he said, "I was just standing in the back of the auditorium, and I heard God speak to me for the first time. He told me that baseball should not be my priority because He wants me to become a pastor." Now, when I heard that, tears started flooding down *my* face. I knew he had experienced a divine interruption.

At the time, I could not stop thinking about his words, "I heard God speak to me for the first time." Of course, Spencer did not mean that God had spoken to him in an audible voice. He was simply acknowledging that he had heard God's quiet whisper to his heart and mind. As a Christian young man, he had grown up in church. He had heard many sermons and teachings about hearing the voice of God. Now for the very first time he had actually heard God Himself speak; this was the first time he knew for sure that he had heard from heaven.

Sometimes people will ask, "Does God still speak today?" We certainly know that He is still speaking through the Bible, which is His written Word for all to read and hear. Beyond that, we need to learn that we can develop such a sensitivity to the Holy Spirit living on the inside of us that we can readily recognize His voice in our hearts and minds. Jesus declared, "My sheep hear My voice, and I know them, and they follow Me" (John 10:27).

What a mind-blowing thought—our Shepherd knows us by name and He wants to speak to us! Notice the relational intimacy that exists between Jesus and His sheep. First, Jesus knows and speaks to His sheep and, in response, His sheep hear and follow. If God is speaking, then we should want to hear and follow.

Hearing from Heaven involves Sacred Cooperation

Perhaps the best term to describe the relational intimacy between God and human beings is "sacred cooperation." Here we must understand the term *sacred* to mean "dedicated to the divine" and the word *cooperation* to mean "serving together." The sacred cooperation between God and His people means that both parties have committed themselves to "serving together in divine dedication."

Although it may seem simplistic to say so, you and I must develop our spiritual ears in order to perform our part in the process. After all, at least eight times in the gospels we read Jesus' exhortation, "If anyone has ears to hear, let him hear."[1]

What would happen if we decided to develop our spiritual hearing? Would that not make an impact on *everything*—family, work, schedule, social media and much more? What if we learned to hear a "sound from heaven" better than the sounds from our phones, laptops or televisions?

God Will Say It!

The truth is that God desires to speak to us. In Matthew's gospel, a centurion came to Jesus and began to tell Him about his paralyzed servant. Without hesitation, Jesus said that He would come and heal him. Sometimes, we think that we need to beg and plead for Jesus to respond, but this example suggests that Jesus is always readily available to hear and meet our needs.

When Jesus responded so quickly, the centurion received a spiritual epiphany:

"Lord, I am not worthy that You should come under my roof. But only speak a word, and my servant will be healed. For I also am a man under authority, having soldiers under me. And I say

105

to this one, 'Go,' and he goes; and to another, 'Come,' and he comes; and to my servant, 'Do this,' and he does it."

Matthew 8:8–9

The centurion did not need anything other than a word from God. In effect, he said, "Lord, just say it, and my servant will be healed." Afterward, Jesus turned to the crowd and said: "Assuredly, I say to you, I have not found such great faith, not even in Israel!" (Matthew 8:10).

Why do we so often hesitate? Why do we question God's word to us? When God whispers, "Talk to your neighbor and share your faith," too often we make excuses. ("But Lord, I am about to go to the grocery store and just don't have time.") Or, if we feel that God may be telling us, "Give that waitress a one-hundred-dollar tip," our natural reasoning causes us to object. ("Lord, does she really need a one-hundred-dollar tip?") The pattern is obvious: God speaks, but we question what He tells us. Often, God will say it, but we will question it.

In the story, Jesus turned toward the crowd—which meant that He turned away from the centurion's house. This did not mean that He wanted to ignore the centurion's plea for help; instead He wanted to affirm the belief that His word was enough. After all, it was by His word and not by His touch that the servant was healed. We marvel at the centurion's faith, which in the end tells us that what God says is always more important than what we see. Or simply stated, God's word is performed when He says it and not when we see it.

This is why "name it and claim it" theology does not really work. Sure, you can lay your hands on a new car and claim it, but it will not become yours unless God says so. We cannot expect to get whatever we see and claim; we will get only what God says. You can name and claim a new job, but whether or not you get it depends upon what God says. Therefore, we must start by listening. And "if anyone has ears to hear, let him hear."

I am sure that you have heard sincere people say, "God said it. . . . I believe it. . . . That settles it." That catchy statement may sound good to our ears, but I find it misleading. Think about it: If God said it, then that settles it. Period. Whether we *believe* it or not does not change the fact that God will say it and then display it.

God Will Say It and Then Display It!

In Scripture, the revelation of a thing often comes before the manifestation of the thing. A revelation from God will come before a manifestation from God. God will reveal something in word and then manifest it in deed. The word will come before the work.

The word *revelation* in the Greek text happens to be the word *apakalupsis*, which is the derivative root of our English word *apocalyptic*. Have you ever considered that God's revelation is really apocalyptic? It points to the future in a decisive way. The *apakalupsis* or apocalyptic nature of God's Word rolls back the curtain to reveal a glimpse into His divine plan for our day and time.

Walk through the pages of the Book of all books and list all of the examples of how God said it and then displayed it. He said it—"Let there be light." And then He displayed it: "And there was light" (Genesis 1:3). He said it—"For unto us a Child is born, unto us a Son is given; and the government will be upon His shoulder" (Isaiah 9:6). And then He displayed it: "But when the fullness of time was come, God sent forth His Son" (Galatians 4:4). He said it—"Behold, I send the Promise of My Father upon you; but tarry in the city of Jerusalem until you are endued with power from on high" (Luke 24:49). And then He displayed it: "And when the day of Pentecost had fully come . . . they were all filled with the Holy Spirit" (Acts 2:1, 4). He said it, as He did to the centurion—"Go your way; and as you have believed, so let it be done for you" (Matthew 8:13), and then He displayed it: "And his servant was healed that same hour" (Matthew 8:13).

God's word precedes God's work. Prophetic revelation precedes divine manifestation.

Hearing from Heaven Involves Active Cooperation

Sacred cooperation eventually moves into active cooperation. What we hear from heaven drives us to action. It is noteworthy that after Jesus healed one paralyzed man (see Matthew 8), He was confronted by another paralytic (see Matthew 9). In this situation, the house in which Jesus was teaching had become so full of people that a small group of friends (four friends, according to Mark 2) decided that the only way they could get their paralyzed buddy to Jesus was to lower him through a hole in the roof on a stretcher. Can you imagine what it was like: You and many others are packed shoulder-to-shoulder inside the house while Jesus teaches about the Kingdom. Suddenly a commotion begins overhead. *What is that? Is somebody up there on the roof?* Then all of a sudden, straw and dried mud begin to fall from the ceiling onto your head and clothes, and the sun glints down through a hole right in front of Jesus.

When the stretcher of the paralyzed man came down through the roof and rested in front of Jesus, He would not have flinched or scolded the man's friends for the way they disrupted His teaching and made such an insufferable mess. He would have ignored all that because He could see the faith of the four friends. In truth, their energetic efforts had provided an opportunity for their paralyzed friend to experience healing. Talk about active cooperation! It was not the faith of the paralytic that catalyzed Christ's response; it was the faith of a few good friends.

I wonder how many wounded people today could benefit from the cooperation of their family and friends to help them more actively seek healing.

God Will Say It and Then Display It When You Hear It

Notice what happened during the exchange between Jesus and the paralytic:

> When Jesus saw their faith, He said to the paralytic, "Son, be of good cheer; your sins are forgiven you." And at once some of the scribes said within themselves, "This Man blasphemes!" But Jesus, knowing their thoughts, said, "Why do you think evil in your hearts?"
>
> Matthew 9:2–4

It is important to recognize the source of what we hear, as the text stresses. Though the paralytic heard from Jesus, the scribes were hearing only their own thoughts: "And at once some of the scribes *said within themselves* . . ." How often do we miss out on hearing from heaven because we interject our own thoughts?

Of course, you might be wondering, "How can I know whether what I hear comes from myself or from God?" Oftentimes you can discern the difference when you recognize that what you hear from God will likely not appeal to your flesh. For instance, in the example above, to give the waitress a one-hundred-dollar tip is probably not an idea that would naturally originate in your own mind; therefore, it is more likely to have been initiated directly by God. Most thoughts that come from God appeal to your spirit while most thoughts that arise from your own consciousness appeal to your flesh.

Jesus could read the thoughts of the scribes ("This Man blasphemes!"). After He exposed the fact that He knew what they were thinking, He closed in on them with a rhetorical question, asking, "For which is easier, to say, 'Your sins are forgiven you,' or to say, 'Arise and walk'?" (Matthew 9:5).

The religious leaders would have found the command "arise and walk" to have been much more acceptable; they believed that someone who is especially anointed by God could perform signs and wonders. But to them, "Your sins are forgiven you" was an over-the-top statement, since forgiveness of sin can only be offered by God Himself.

Even today, many people feel the same. It is easier for them to hear Jesus say, "arise and walk" than "your sins are forgiven," because the former addresses an immediate physical need while the latter addresses an invisible internal condition. "Arise and walk" impacts your right now while "Your sins are forgiven you" impacts your forever.

In truth, God wants to heal you from the inside out. He wants to heal you spiritually more than He does physically. He wants to impact your eternity more than your earthly existence and your "forever" more than your "now." Even as you read these pages, be open to hearing something from God, perhaps for the first time, that has the capacity to change your destiny. It will come not from inside yourself but from heaven. "If anyone has ears to hear, let him hear."

Why does the Scripture not say, "If anyone has eyes to see, let him see"? Because if you have spiritual ears, you will have spiritual eyes. When you begin to hear things from God, you will begin to see things from God. Whatever you hear from heaven, you will see on earth. Scripture also tells us: "So then faith comes by hearing, and hearing by the word of God" (Romans 10:17).

Here is the problem: Just like the scribes and Pharisees, we continue to hear the wrong things. The Bible identifies this as "carnal mindedness": "For to be carnally minded is death, but to be spiritually minded is life and peace" (Romans 8:6). Your carnal mind will seek to keep you spiritually weak by saying, "But you're still paralyzed and can't go anywhere." But your spiritual mind will say, "That's not what I heard; I heard, 'Arise, take up your bed, and go to your house'" (Matthew 9:6).

Your carnal mind will try to convince you, "You're still in a mess, and that mountain stands in the way." But your spiritual mind will say, "That's not what I heard; I heard, 'Whoever says to this mountain, "Be removed and be cast into the sea," and does not doubt in his heart, but believes that those things he says will be done, he will have whatever he says'" (Mark 11:23).

Your carnal mind will seek to discourage you by declaring, "Your promise will never come true—you're further away today than when you first started." But your spiritual mind will say, "That's not what I heard; I heard, 'I know whom I have believed and am persuaded that He is able to keep what I have committed to Him until that Day'" (2 Timothy 1:12).

Your carnal mind will try to motivate you toward financial surrender, saying, "But you've got too much month at the end of your money." But your spiritual mind will say, "That's not what I heard; I heard, 'And my God shall supply all your need according to His riches in glory by Christ Jesus'" (Philippians 4:19).

Your carnal mind will point toward your loss, "Your son or daughter will never be saved." But your spiritual mind will say, "That's not what I heard; I heard, 'Train up a child in the way he should go, and when he is old he will not depart from it'" (Proverbs 22:6). Faith is a spiritual muscle. To strengthen it, we must redirect our carnal minds toward God's Word. "If anyone has ears to hear, let him hear."

Notice what happened when the paralytic was healed. As it turned out, the religious leaders were actually the ones responsible for initiating the healing. When Jesus said, "But that you may know that the Son of Man has power on earth to forgive sins" and then He said to the paralytic, "Arise, take up your bed, and go to your house" (Matthew 9:6), He was saying, in essence, "Just so you religious leaders recognize that I am who I say I am—the Messiah, the Son of God who bears authority to forgive sin—I will go ahead and complete on the outside what I have already started on the inside."

God Will Say It and Display It, When You Hear It and Declare It

There is power in a verbal declaration. From the time my children were in the womb, I have made declarations over them and my family by praying: "Heavenly Father, cover my family with Your blood. Let Your guardian angels encamp around about us. Holy Spirit, rise up within us. I pray that we will be strong in our adversity and humble in our success. Help us to walk in divine healing and divine health. Prepare, position and propel us into Your purposes and plans for our lives. Help us to be a godly family that makes a worldwide difference. Amen."

Scripture repeatedly teaches that words set off a chain reaction that is either positive or negative. Unfortunately, we more often see the negative than the positive. Dad comes home tired and frustrated, and he yells at Mom. Mom then yells at the older brother. The older brother then yells at the younger sister. The younger sister then kicks the dog. The dog then bites the cat. The cat then scratches the baby. The baby then bites the head off of her Barbie doll. As a matter of fact, it might have been easier and quicker if Dad had come home and had just bitten the head off the Barbie doll himself! The point is that our words create a chain reaction. What we say can make us happy or sad, healthy or unhealthy, wise or foolish. The words we utter can build people up or tear people down; they can get us hired or fired.

Why do you think the children of Israel wandered in the wilderness for forty years? Why did an eleven-day journey take them four decades? We can overspiritualize it and explain, "They had a slave's mentality that needed to change" or "God needed to prepare them for the Promised Land." Even though these excuses may have some truth, the bottom line is that they wandered for forty years because they were complainers, and they came up with many excuses: "The Canaanites are like giants, and they will crush us like grasshoppers." "We have only come to the wilderness to die; oh, that we could go back to Egypt." "How come we don't have meat to eat or water to drink?" God had already given them the land (see Numbers 13:2), but they were not able to possess it because their future had been confined in a prison cell created by their own words.

I sometimes wonder if our mouths need to be redeemed by the blood of Jesus. Our grandparents may have washed their children's mouths out with soap, but God does much more. The Scripture says that we are sanctified and "washed by the cleansing of God's word" (Ephesians 5:26 NLT).

The paralytic took this truth a step further, since his declarations were nonverbal "action steps." He did not declare anything with his voice. Instead, he made a declaration through his actions: "And he arose and departed to his house" (Matthew 9:7). He did not neglect to do what he had been told to do.

The paralytic's declarations occurred nonverbally as he stood up and walked home. So, too, ours (whether verbal or nonverbal) should result in action. The book of James makes this clear:

> Can't you see that *faith without good deeds is useless*? Don't you remember that our ancestor Abraham was shown to be right with God by his actions when he offered his son Isaac on the altar? You see, his faith and his actions worked together. His actions made his faith complete.
>
> James 2:21–22 NLT, emphasis added

113

The inference is clear: Faith without action is no faith at all. Declarations without deeds are incomplete. We can "say it," but if we do not "display it," then all we have are dead words.

In Abraham's case, he heard God instruct him to offer his son as a sacrifice, but he still needed to declare it through his actions. Would Abraham trust God with his most valued treasure? When we read on in the biblical narrative, we discover the answer: Abraham believed God, and his faith was placed in a heavenly account (see James 2:23). Just as Abraham lifted the knife over his son, he *heard* something! A ram was caught in the thicket, and it provided the perfect sacrifice for Abraham instead of his own son. From that moment on, that place was called Jehovah Jireh, "which means 'the LORD will provide'" (Genesis 22:14 NLT). The key for Abraham and for us today involves our "active cooperation" with God because *God will say it and display it, when we hear it and declare it.*

Thankfully, today we do not have to wonder what God's Word looks and sounds like, because Jesus has come: "The Word [Jesus] became human and made his home among us. He was full of unfailing love and faithfulness. And we have seen his glory, the glory of the Father's one and only Son" (John 1:14 NLT). God declared His Word through His Son, Jesus Christ, which meant that hearing from heaven had not been unveiled through a thing but instead through a Person.

When Jesus Christ made His home among us, He began to express His glory or nature to us. In effect, the disciples and others who saw Him in action began to hear from heaven through His every word and deed.

- The Word turned the water into wine at the wedding of Cana.
- The Word put mud on the blind man's eyes and healed him.

- The Word fed more than five thousand people with a boy's lunch.
- The Word delivered a man from a legion of demons.
- The Word healed ten lepers on the way to Jericho.
- The Word raised Jairus' daughter from the dead.
- The Word bled and died on a wooden cross.
- The Word rose from the dead on the third day.

Through every verbal and nonverbal declaration, the Word had been revealed through the Person of Jesus Christ. More importantly today, the Word continues to be revealed through Him. When you find the Way, you do not find a thing; you find Christ. When you receive the Truth, you do not receive a thing; you receive Christ. When you experience the Life, you do not experience a thing; you experience Christ.

Recently, I heard about a social-media-driven competition between Chick-fil-A and Popeyes. Everyone had a strong opinion in relation to whose chicken sandwich is better. In the heat of this battle, only one of those chicken establishments ran out of chicken—Popeyes. Fortunately, when we need to hear from heaven, we do not ever need to worry—we will never, ever run out of God's Word. He is always faithful to say it and display it when we hear it and declare it.

Personal CHALLENGE

When you hear from heaven, you really hear from Him, and it can happen at any time. He can speak to you while you wait for a red light, when you sit in a coffee shop or while you attend a school event. He can talk to you in a board room, hospital room, classroom or bedroom. Or, as in the case of my son Spencer, He can whisper to you in the back of a church auditorium.

A pastor friend told me about a woman who was in a crack house. In the midst of her mess, God showed up and said, "Choose you this day—life or death." She was as high as a kite, but she immediately called her dad, who picked her up and took her to church. That night, she surrendered her life to Christ and has served Him ever since. So, what do you hear from heaven right now? "If anyone has ears to hear, let him hear."

In the two stories of the paralyzed men, both men were paralyzed in their bodies. But sometimes, you can be paralyzed mentally and spiritually as well. Whatever paralysis you may be experiencing, here is the good news: God wants to trade your paralysis for His peace.

And just in case you feel as though a barrier or a ceiling blocks you from God, I believe four friends or a centurion can come into your life and ensure that you get to Him. Sometimes, God's divine interruption takes the form of His putting the right people in the right place at the right time. When we finally get through the obstacle and find Jesus, He will heal us from the inside out.

Personal REFLECTION

1. Have you ever heard from God? If so, when was the last time and what did He say?

2. Unlike the centurion who took Jesus at His word, do you sometimes question what you hear from God? Think of an example of this in your own life.

3. When the paralytic was lowered through the roof, the religious leaders did not understand what was happening. They continued to hear from themselves instead of

Jesus. How do you discern between hearing from yourself and hearing from the Lord?

4. Have you thought about the notion that God wants to heal you from the inside out? How would this make a significant difference to you?

5. Do you make declarations of God's truth that are not only verbal but also nonverbal? If so, give some examples.

Personal PRAYER

Heavenly Father, I desperately need to hear from heaven. I desire to hear and obey Your voice. Help me to discern between my carnal mind and Your word. I choose to respond with sensitive spiritual ears. I want to live with a renewed commitment to make both verbal and nonverbal declarations of the truth. I recognize that Your Word is not a thing but a Person. You are the Word! And I hear You, Lord! Thank You for Your divine interruption in my life so that You can speak to my heart. In Jesus' name, Amen.

Group CHALLENGE

Much like the two paralytics Jesus met, we have the opportunity to hear and respond to the Word. We can remain paralyzed physically, mentally, emotionally or spiritually, or we can be healed. However, sometimes the obstacle to our healing remains in our ability to hear and discern God's voice. Our spiritual ears need to be further developed. Allow the biblical stories about how Jesus healed the two paralytics to provide a launching point for a deeper group discussion about hearing from heaven.

1. Have you ever heard from God? If so, when was the last time and what did He say?

2. Unlike the centurion who took Jesus at His Word, do you sometimes question what you hear? Do you struggle with how to know if it is God who speaks to you? Provide an example of this in your own life.

3. When the paralytic was lowered through the roof, the religious leaders were quick to limit their response to only their own opinions. They heard from themselves instead of from Jesus. How do you discern between your own inner voice and that of the Lord?

4. Have you thought about the notion that God wants to heal you from the inside out? Discuss the implications of this and how it impacts you and others.

5. Discuss your thoughts about the following:
   a. your carnal mind (which will seek to overwhelm you)
   b. your spiritual mind (which can be encouraged by a word from God)

6. When the paralyzed man was lowered through the roof, this bold action made a nonverbal declaration about his faith in Jesus. Discuss verbal and nonverbal declarations. What is the difference between them?

7. The Scripture declares, "So the Word became human and made his home among us. He was full of unfailing love and faithfulness. And we have seen his glory, the glory of the Father's one and only Son" (John 1:14 NLT). Discuss the notion that the Word is "a person" and not "a thing."

8. God can speak to you at any time and in any place. Do you hear His voice right now? If so, what is He saying?

7

Enlist as a First Responder

I . . . beseech you to walk worthy of the calling with
which you were called.

Ephesians 4:1

Some of the greatest heroes of the 21st century are first
responders—those who show up immediately in the
midst of crisis. When the coronavirus pandemic began,
first responders across the globe stepped up to care for the suffering. One doctor, Luigi Cavanna, who was the head of the
oncology ward at Guglielmo da Saliceto hospital in Piacenza,
Italy, decided to visit people in their homes. He shared:

I realized we shouldn't be waiting for the COVID-19 patients
to get to the hospital. We needed to go to people's homes. . . .

I started to drive around the area surrounding the Piacenza with my staff. . . . So far we have visited almost 300 patients. . . . I'm one of those doctors who could have retired, but I chose not to. I'm not an alarmist by nature, but this is a tragedy. And we all need to do what we can, and what we can do best, to deal with it.[1]

How often do we see a first responder like Dr. Cavanna race toward a crisis to save a life or make a difference where it is needed most? First responders enlist quickly to serve others in their time of need, and most often they do not take any concern for their own lives. As Dennis Canale, who served the NYPD ESU (Emergency Service Unit) for sixteen years, stated:

Unfortunately, I've been through 9/11, I worked down at Ground Zero for several months. I've watched my colleagues as first responders dive right in, no regard for their own safety, just for the wellbeing of others.[2]

Certainly, words seem inadequate to express appreciation for those who serve on the frontlines of their communities.

In much the same way, did you know that God enlists first responders for His Kingdom? One day, as Jesus traveled through the towns and villages around Galilee, He saw a multitude of people who suffered with illness and other difficulties. Because of it, He was deeply moved with compassion, and He told His disciples: "The harvest truly is plentiful, but the laborers are few. Therefore pray the Lord of the harvest to send out laborers into His harvest" (Matthew 9:37–38).

Jesus recognized the size of the assignment and the need for more workers—those who would serve in the harvest field of the Kingdom—so He challenged His followers not only to enlist as first responders but also to recruit others.

The apostle Paul reinforced this idea when he wrote, "I, therefore, the prisoner of the Lord, beseech you to walk worthy of the calling with which you were called" (Ephesians 4:1). Paul had experienced a divine interruption. When he was still known as Saul, he thirsted for the blood of Christ-followers, but one day, a brilliant light overwhelmed him until he fell to the ground (see Acts 9:3–4). Jesus Christ spoke to him in the middle of the road, and he was captured by His calling. Afterward, everything changed. Saul enlisted as a first responder in the Kingdom of God, and his name was changed to Paul.

Do you know what it means to experience a divine interruption and be captured by your calling? In at least one way, I do. When I was eight years old, I attended a kids' camp in the state of Michigan. There I was captured by Christ. I found myself on my hands and knees on a cement floor while the Holy Spirit spoke to my heart with regard to preaching the Gospel to the nations of the world. Of course, I did not understand the comprehensive nature of what God had said to me, but I remember that I cried out and passionately declared as well as an eight-year-old boy can, "Lord, I'll be what You want me to be, do what You want me to do and go where You want me to go."

But after my experience, much like Paul, I was confronted by a choice. Would I accept and pursue God's call for my life? Or, would I follow my own plans? As I have pondered these questions throughout my life, I have become convinced that God is actually more concerned with our availability than with our ability. He does not look for the most talented people, although He certainly appreciates them. And He does not seek for people who may be inclined to change the words of the song, "I surrender all" to "I surrender some." No, He chooses people who will surrender all for His call, make themselves available to do His will and enlist as "first responders" in His Kingdom.

Have You Been Called?

If you are a Christian, you have been called by God, whether you realize it or not. And that means that every Christian is in the midst of a discovery process with regard to his or her God-given calling. Paul told the Corinthians: "But as God hath distributed to every man, as *the Lord hath called every one*, so let him walk. And so ordain I in all churches" (1 Corinthians 7:17 KJV, emphasis added).

What has God distributed to every man? And what did Paul ordain in all the churches? Simply this, that everyone has a calling, and everyone should walk it out. To make it personal, you have a calling, and you should walk it out. And your calling has not come from a spouse or a boss or a pastor as much as it has come from the Divine Being who created you.

That is why Paul put it this way, "I, therefore, the prisoner of the Lord, beseech you to *walk worthy of the calling* with which you were called" (Ephesians 4:1, emphasis added). He addressed that to the Ephesian Christians and, by extension, to anyone who has been called to become a citizen in the Kingdom of God. Paul pleaded with all of us through his letter to the Ephesians: "Walk worthy of God's calling. Do not follow your own agenda."

Unfortunately, personal agendas and preferences can all too often distract us from our calling. A young boy was on his way to church with two quarters from his mother. She told him that he could spend one quarter however he pleased and put the other in the church offering plate. But as he ran down the sidewalk toward the church, he tripped and fell. One quarter rolled out of his hand and into the sewer. When he saw what had happened, he said, "Oops! God, there goes Your quarter."[3] In such unexpected situations, God seems to get our leftovers. Our agenda takes precedence over His.

From the very beginning, humankind has struggled with the oops-God-there-goes-Your-quarter syndrome. When God placed Adam in the Garden, He gave him a calling to tend to the plants and animals and to maintain fellowship with Him (see Genesis 2:15). Sadly, Adam tended to his own agenda: He ate some of the fruit of the one tree from which he had been restricted. In the process, the Garden of Adam's calling (which was a calling to all of humankind) had to be abandoned. The only way God could restore it was to send His Son. The actions of the "first Adam" turned the Garden into a wasteland, but the "second Adam" set in motion a plan to turn the wasteland back into a Garden. In essence, Jesus Christ became the ultimate Gardener and restored the calling of Adam to his descendants. Jesus put it beautifully, saying, "Abide in Me, and I in you. As the branch cannot bear fruit of itself, unless it abides in the vine, neither can you, unless you abide in Me" (John 15:4).

Interestingly, when Jesus rose from the dead and Mary Magdalene was the first person to see Him, who did she think she saw? The *gardener* (see John 20:15)! This is no coincidence. When you meet the resurrected Christ, you, too, will see Him as the Gardener of your calling. And just as He did with Mary Magdalene, He will provide instructions: "Go to my brethren and say to them . . ." (John 20:17). Or as He spoke to the apostle Paul on the road to Damascus, He will capture you and initiate your calling: "I am Jesus, the one you are persecuting! Now get up and go into the city, and you will be told what you must do" (Acts 9:5–6 NLT).

I do not mean to suggest that we persecute Jesus every time we give Him only the leftovers of our lives, but I do suggest that we, like Paul, should enlist as first responders. You and I should prepare ourselves to hear His instructions for our lives so that we can proceed to walk worthy of His calling.

What Is Your Calling?

First, we need to understand what to look for when we say "calling." How can we walk worthy of our calling if the term is incomprehensible to us?

In the Old Testament, one's calling seemed to be more of an invitation to live in relationship with God; it was about "being." God called the world, humankind, and the nation of Israel into being. However, a New Testament calling includes more of a summons to serve God in a unique way and time; it is about "doing." Today, we have been called to be God's own children, and God's call for relationship elicits a call for service.[4]

The divine nature of one's calling mandates a personal response to a comprehensive relationship. When we enter into a true relationship with God, we must give both our ability and our availability back to Him. Note well: *Your calling is to take what God has given you and to give it back to Him.*

If you are creative in graphic design, you give it back to God. If you are talented in business, you give it back to God. If you are excellent in teaching, you give it back to God. Whatever abilities God has given you, give them back to Him. Let's unpack this further. How do your God-given abilities fit into your God-given calling?

Born with God-Given Abilities

When you were born, you received God-given abilities. God placed certain gifts and abilities within your physical DNA. God did that! "In his grace, God has given us different gifts for doing certain things well" (Romans 12:6 NLT). Have you ever thought about the fact that you were conceived by God long before you were conceived by your parents?

Oftentimes your abilities are shaped by your God-given physique. How can a basketball player become a horse jockey, or a horse jockey compete in sumo wrestling? Basketball players were not created to ride racehorses, and horse jockeys were not created to wrestle. Some people have the form and physique that will allow them to pump iron and become bodybuilders, while others do not. Some have the grace and finesse that will allow them to become ballerinas while others could pirouette for hours on end and achieve nothing more than chronic dizziness.

God designed every creature with certain abilities; each one will excel in certain areas. A duck is meant to swim. A rabbit is meant to run. A squirrel is meant to climb, and an eagle is meant to fly. You are meant to be you and nobody else will do. In one of his best-known essays, "Self-Reliance," Ralph Waldo Emerson once wrote, "There is a time in every man's education when he arrives at the conviction that . . . imitation is suicide, that he must take himself for better, for worse."[5]

Have you ever sat in a mall or another public place so that you could watch the parade of people as they walk by? No two are the same. Our Creator God loves creativity and variety, and every single one of the billions of people who exist or who have ever existed on this planet is uniquely different.

Biologists tell us that each of us has 46 chromosomes—23 from our father and 23 from our mother. Those chromosomes are invaluable, because they determine everything from the color of your eyes to the number of hairs on your head.

Consider how absolutely unique you are:

The mathematical probability that you would get the exact twenty-three chromosomes you got from your mother is .5 to the twenty-third power. That's 1 in 10 million. But the same is true for the twenty-three chromosomes you got from your father. So if you multiply those two together, the probability that you would be you is 1 in 100 trillion. But you also have to factor in that your parents' chromosomal history had the same probability, and their parents, and their parents' parents. My point? You are incalculably unique.[6]

Sociologists have also shown that the average person has between five hundred and seven hundred different kinds of abilities.[7] Some people are good at computers, while others are good with mechanical operations. Some are good with numbers, while others are good with words. Different people are good with music or ideas or thought processes. Some have the ability to cook, draw, speak, research, landscape or build. Those abilities are not accidental, but creational. They are God-given abilities.

And yet, those abilities are not the same as your calling. Paul did not tell you to walk worthy of your *abilities* but to walk worthy of your *calling*. When you were born, you received God-given abilities, but when you were born again, you received a God-given calling.

Born Again with a God-Given Calling

When you experience salvation (or being born again) in Christ, the purpose of your life changes. For a living, Peter, Andrew, James and John used to fish for fish, but after they were born again they started fishing for men. Paul persecuted the Gospel, but after he was born again he preached the Gospel. In the same way, after salvation, your life shifts from a career to a calling.

We must recognize the difference; a career and a calling are not one and the same. Now, I know these notions are often confusing, especially for people who are not Christ-followers, so allow me to offer some clarification. Once you are born again, your career and calling become two separate entities, because your decision to follow the Lord Jesus Christ has automatically enlisted you as a first responder in the Kingdom of God. Your decision to follow Christ sets you on a course to do something beyond merely following in a career.

A career makes the world a better place, while a calling makes the Kingdom a better place.

A career allows you to do something of earthly significance while a calling allows you to do something of eternal significance.

As a Christian who is called to walk worthy of your calling, you are now asked to connect your career to your calling in the Kingdom of God. A non-Christian who works in marketing can probably make the world a better a place, but a Christian who works in marketing is called to use his or her marketing skills to make the Kingdom of God a better place. A non-Christian businessperson can provide deliverables to people and make the world a better place in the process, but a Christian businessperson is called to provide deliverables that make the Kingdom a better place. A non-Christian teacher can teach kids to read and write and make the world a better place, but a Christian teacher is called to use that teaching gift to go further—to accomplish something of eternal significance.

This is mind-boggling, and the implications are staggering. Countless Christians all around the world have not recognized this distinction between a career and a calling. Regrettably, they have pursued careers but have missed out on their callings. By serving in a career to make the world a better place, they may discover too late that they were climbing a ladder of success that leaned against the wrong building.

I will never forget the schoolteacher who approached me after church one Sunday. I had shared several of these thoughts in my sermon that morning, and she said she had trouble wrapping her mind around the implications for her own life. She shared her heartfelt feelings that her career as an elementary school teacher was just too exhausting to allow her also to volunteer to teach children within the church congregation. As lovingly as possible, I questioned her concerning her willingness to use her God-given gifts to make an earthly impact but not to go beyond that to make an eternal impact. She reconsidered and started teaching children about the Lord at church in addition to teaching them weekdays in school.

Your God-given calling is not the same as your occupational career, although the two may seem to overlap. People who have wonderful entrepreneurial skills and serve their communities with excellence need to connect their leadership prowess to God and His Kingdom so that they can follow their God-given calling. Those who serve as doctors and nurses in health-care facilities, who care for people who suffer with physical illnesses, have tremendous gifts and abilities to offer to God and His Kingdom. Even remaining at exactly the same jobs, they may be able to do something of eternal significance.

To walk worthy of your calling, you must connect your career to the Kingdom of God. When you choose to do this, you partner with God. This will both close the distance between you and God and make an impact on others around you.

The real work of the Church does not take place when we lift up the cross in the church house; it happens when we lift it up in the marketplace. When Jesus was crucified, He did not carry His cross through the back alleys of the city; He carried His cross through the very center, where all the commerce and foot traffic were concentrated. In the case of the schoolteacher I mentioned above, I did not intend to convince her to become another volunteer (though such service is certainly welcomed in the church). Instead, I simply wanted to challenge her to be more intentional about the use of her gifts and abilities so that they would further magnify the name of Jesus Christ. In truth, we must exalt the cross of Christ in the chambers of city hall, in the classrooms of our educational institutions, in the rooms of hospital and health-care facilities and in the recording studios of our entertainment centers and everywhere that we work and play.

Recently, I heard the interesting statistic that approximately three percent of all church attendees will receive financial support as a result of their work in a local church. Though this may seem to be a discouraging piece of data, I was excited about it because I realized that the other 97 percent of all church attendees must have the opportunity to make the Lord Jesus known in every other sector of society. If God only called the three percent, the world would never be reached by the love of Christ. But since the harvest is abundant, He did not call only the three percent; He also called the other 97 percent to go into the world and make a difference for the Kingdom.

When Paul was captured by his calling, he changed from a Pharisee who continually persecuted Christians. He plugged his ability and availability into the Kingdom of God. He began to travel to places such as Athens, a skeptical city filled with idolatry, where he could use his extensive education and oratory skill to take on the philosophers and intellectuals in his powerful sermon about the unknown God (see Acts 17:23). His natural boldness and assertiveness served him well when he preached before Christ-hating Jews, Tertullus the governor, Felix his successor, King Agrippa and those of Caesar's household. Paul did not walk worthy of his calling because he was an extraordinary Christian; he became an extraordinary Christian because he connected his gifts to the Kingdom.

How Do You Walk Worthy of Your Calling?

Once you discover the "what" of your calling, then the looming challenge of "how" rises to the surface. How do you walk worthy of your calling? In his book *The Call*, Os Guinness wrote, "Calling is not only a matter of being and doing what we are but also of becoming what we are not yet but are called by God to be."[8] In other words, you begin a spiritual journey that shifts your attention from the person you are to the person you need to become in God. You embark on a journey from the "now" to the "not yet." Frederick Buechner similarly states: "Buried in me too are all the people I have not been yet but might be someday."[9] To walk worthy of your calling involves a progressive voyage of discovery toward the person you are becoming in God.

However, inevitably all of us will run into obstacles. Allow me to elaborate upon four barriers that may present themselves as we journey toward the discovery of that person God has destined us to become.

Overcome Personal Pain

In professional sports, players are sometimes placed on the disabled list because they are hurt and cannot perform. They may be on the disabled list for a few days or an entire season, but their personal pain keeps them out of the game. As Christians, we must monitor our personal heartache and pain to ensure that we do not end up on the disabled list for an extended period of time, and if we do, we must do our absolute best to get back in the game as soon as possible.

If anyone could have given up on their calling because of personal pain, it should have been the apostle Paul. He wrote:

> I've worked much harder, been jailed more often, beaten up more times than I can count, and at death's door time after time. I've been flogged five times with the Jews' thirty-nine lashes, beaten by Roman rods three times, pummeled with rocks once. I've been shipwrecked three times, and immersed in the open sea for a night and a day. In hard traveling year in and year out, I've had to ford rivers, fend off robbers, struggle with friends, struggle with foes. I've been at risk in the city, at risk in the country, endangered by desert sun and sea storm, and betrayed by those I thought were my brothers. I've known drudgery and hard labor, many a long

and lonely night without sleep, many a missed meal, blasted by
the cold, naked to the weather. And that's not the half of it, when
you throw in the daily pressures and anxieties of all the churches.

2 Corinthians 11:23–28 MESSAGE

Amazingly, this is not even a complete list of his sufferings, because Paul's letters to the Corinthians were written before his imprisonment in Jerusalem and subsequent shipwreck in the Mediterranean on his way to Rome. After he wrote this letter, Paul would go on to be imprisoned three more times! But regardless of his circumstances, he did not allow his personal pain to keep him on the disabled list. He continued to walk worthy of his calling.

Overcome Displaced Priorities

The demands of life can fill your schedule with more temporal concerns than you realize. You can become so heavily invested in your climb up the corporate latter, the maintenance of your calendar or your enjoyment of the latest fad that you remain distracted from any attempt to walk worthy of your calling.

The rich young ruler we read about in Luke 18 certainly comes to mind. Like Paul, he had grown up "in religion." He had kept all the commandments and had enjoyed a measure of wealth and prosperity. But when he sought out the rabbi Jesus, his displaced priorities kept him from accepting his calling, and he walked away from Christ.

Of course, "The gifts and calling of God are irrevocable" (Romans 11:29), or "without repentance" as the King James version puts it. When the rich young ruler walked away, God did not remove his gifts. If someone has an excellent singing voice, God is not so petty as to take it from the person, saying, "Well, if you won't sing for the Kingdom, then I will revoke

131

your gift." Displaced priorities generally do not damage your gift, but they can certainly diminish your calling.

Overcome Relational Offense

Recently, I heard an interesting story about a woman who posted an advertisement in the newspaper. She had offered to sell a new Mercedes for fifty dollars. When a young man responded to the advertisement in disbelief, the woman shared that when her husband had left her for a younger woman, he had informed her that she could have everything except the Mercedes. He had asked her to sell the vehicle and then turn over the amount received in exchange. Hence her spiteful asking price of fifty dollars! Although this woman's actions may seem justifiable, they reveal a vengeful motivation. With God's help, we can overcome any relational offense.

Paul experienced both sides of a relational offense with his young protégé John Mark. Paul and Barnabas had taken the young man on their first missionary journey, but for some reason, he returned home early (see Acts 13:13). Paul felt abandoned and offended, and he was determined that John Mark should not accompany them on their next journey, while Barnabas insisted that he should tag along. This caused Paul to hold a grievance against Barnabas, and it became so pronounced that Paul and Barnabas had to go their separate ways for a while.

We are glad to see that they did reconcile later, and Paul's offense did not sideline his calling (or theirs). Yet that is not always the case. Too many people fail to reconcile their differences with others, and consequently they stifle their callings.

Overcome Low Self-Esteem

How many Christians end up doing very little for God because they struggle with a lack of self-esteem? They feel that their contribution to the Kingdom is so insignificant that they do not even warrant an invitation to the party. While everyone else is at Cinderella's ball, they are out tending their father's sheep. While their brothers are lined up in their suits and ties to party with the prophet and their sisters all wait for their dance with the Prince, they are picking burrs out of their sheep's wool.

Have you ever felt that way? If so, allow me to remind you that God has not forgotten you. While others may look at your outward appearance, God looks at your heart. Everyone else may celebrate at the party, but God sees you over there crunching those numbers, swinging that hammer or bathing those elderly people because they cannot do it for themselves. You may not see it yet, but God has already prepared for your arrival as He did when David was out tending his father's flock of sheep.

The prophet Samuel said to Jesse, David's father, "Send and bring him [David]. For we will not sit down till he comes here" (1 Samuel 16:11). Can you imagine it? Everyone stood at attention when David arrived. His brothers and sisters had put on their Sunday finest and then David walked in, unsightly and still smelling like the sheep. When David walked into the party, all eyes were upon him.

Listen carefully, the whole world awaits the called ones! The harvest is abundant, and the world needs believers to enlist as first responders, people who are intent on becoming the best version of whoever God created them to be, unique in their ability and availability and ready to reveal the greatness of God wherever they go.

Called ones are so captivated by their calling that personal pain, displaced priorities, relational offense or low self-esteem will never keep them from drawing nearer to God.

Perhaps the best illustration of this can be seen when Paul was stoned and left for dead on his first missionary journey:

> Then Jews from Antioch and Iconium came there; and having persuaded the multitudes, they stoned Paul and dragged him out of the city, supposing him to be dead. However, when the disciples gathered around him, he rose up and went into the city. And the next day he departed with Barnabas to Derbe.
>
> Acts 14:19–20

After such an attack, most of us would have fled for our lives. But not Paul. What would cause a man to rise up out of a rock pile of death and return to face the rock-throwers one more time? What would motivate him to rise up again and again and still keep on going? I believe it was because He was absolutely sure of his calling, and he was able to walk worthy of it.

Personal CHALLENGE

When you become a follower of Jesus Christ, you become a card-carrying member of the called ones, and you enlist as a first responder in the Kingdom. At that point, you begin to do something of eternal, not merely earthly, significance.

So, the paramount question remains: What is your calling? Are you walking worthy of it? Are you connecting your ability and availability to the Kingdom? When I was a boy, down on that cement floor at that Michigan camp, I was confronted with a choice. Would I say yes or no? When God summons you to your calling, you can accept or decline. You can run toward it or, like Jonah, you can run away from it. Thankfully, God does not give up easily. He will continue to interrupt the flow of your life and get your attention.

Right now, I want to lay down the gauntlet. It is time to "walk worthy of your calling." Decide to overcome any and all barriers that keep you on the sidelines and out of the game. With the apostle Paul, it is time to make a personal declaration:

> The very credentials these people are waving around as something special, I'm tearing up and throwing out with the trash—along with everything else I used to take credit for. And why? Because of Christ. Yes, all the things I once thought were so important are gone from my life. Compared to the high privilege of knowing Christ Jesus as my Master, firsthand, everything I once thought I had going for me is insignificant—dog dung. I've dumped it all in the trash so that I could embrace Christ and be embraced by him.
>
> Philippians 3:8–9 MESSAGE

Personal EVALUATION

In the example of the apostle Paul we find someone who was captured by his calling. Allow the lessons you have learned in this chapter to compel you to evaluate your own calling and walk worthy of it.

1. The apostle Paul stated, "I . . . the prisoner of the Lord" (Ephesians 4:1). In what way are you a prisoner of the Lord, too? What are the implications for your life?
2. When you were born, you received God-given abilities. List the gifts that you can see in your life.
3. How have you learned to connect your gifts to the Kingdom of God? What would help you do it better?
4. Evaluate whether personal pain, displaced priorities, relational offense or low self-esteem have become obstacles for you.
5. Evaluate whether you are walking worthy of your calling.

135

Personal PRAYER

Heavenly Father, capture my heart with Your calling. There is no doubt that You have created me with gifts, and there is no doubt that You desire for me to connect them to Your Kingdom. I give all that I am and have to You. Personal pain will not keep me out of the game. Displaced priorities will not redirect my time and energy away from You. Relational offense will not disable me. Low self-esteem will not cause me to give up on my calling. I will be what You want me to be, do what You want me to do and go where You want me to go. I submit the garden of my life to You, the ultimate Gardener, and I declare that I will walk worthy of my calling. In Jesus' name, Amen.

Group CHALLENGE

In the example of the apostle Paul, we find someone who was captured by his calling. And just like Paul, any of us can argue with God. But if we truly seek to grow closer to Him, we will allow Him to win the argument every time. Let the lessons you have learned in this chapter assist you in undertaking a "deeper dive" discussion with your group.

1. The apostle Paul stated, "I . . . the prisoner of the Lord" (Ephesians 4:1). Discuss the implications of his statement for all Christians.
2. When you were born, you received God-given abilities. Discuss with each other the gifts that you can identify in your life.
3. What are some of the reasons that people may have a difficult time connecting their gifts to the Kingdom of God?
4. Discuss the difference between God-given gifts and a God-given calling.

5. Discuss the implications of the statistics about the relatively small percentage of church attenders who work for a church, compared to the large percentage who work in secular jobs.

6. Discuss how the following can keep you from walking worthy of your calling:

   a. personal pain

   b. displaced priorities

   c. relational offense

   d. low self-esteem

7. Discuss with each other how you feel you are walking worthy of your calling.

8

Reproduction over the Production

"Go therefore and make disciples of all the nations, baptizing them in the name of the Father and of the Son and of the Holy Spirit, teaching them to observe all things that I have commanded you; and lo, I am with you always, even to the end of the age." Amen.

Matthew 28:19–20

Right before the resurrected Lord ascended to heaven, He gave the disciples some important last-minute instructions. In one of the most penetrating declarations in Scripture, we catch a glimpse of God's global plan for the earth and our role in it:

"Go therefore and make disciples of all the nations, baptizing them in the name of the Father and of the Son and of the Holy Spirit, teaching them to observe all things that I have commanded you; and lo, I am with you always, even to the end of the age." Amen.

Matthew 28:19–20

During the first three centuries of Christianity, churches had only portions of the 27 books of the New Testament and perhaps a copy of the Septuagint, the Greek version of the Old Testament.[1] Believers found the public reading of Scripture vital because they did not own personal copies of the Word of God. Yet, despite this scarcity of Scripture, almost every Christian knew specific parts of the books of Isaiah and Micah. With reference to the book of Isaiah, even the ancient church father Origin asked, "Who does not know this passage?"[2]

Now it shall come to pass in the latter days that the mountain of the LORD's house shall be established on the top of the mountains, and shall be exalted above the hills; and all nations shall flow to it.

Isaiah 2:2

That the mountain of the LORD's house shall be established on the top of the mountains, and shall be exalted above the hills; and peoples shall flow to it. Many nations shall come and say, "Come, and let us go up to the mountain of the LORD."

Micah 4:1–2

The early Christians expected that the mission of Christ would attract all the nations of the world, and even though the call to ascend "the mountain of the Lord" pointed toward a specific place, the emphasis still remained on outreach to all people everywhere.

Oftentimes in today's world, when we talk about "church" we make reference to a specific location. We point to the intersection of Interstate 25 and Highway 156 or mention a well-known spot close to the church building. Though churches today are known for gathering at a certain location each week, the Church is not really a building or a steeple or a place at all. The Church is a people! If we allow ourselves to view the Church only as a location, we can develop the mindset of "going to church" or "doing church" rather than "being the Church." Church can come to mean the events that are held inside the church facilities rather than a people outside the premises. In too many ways, our emphasis can become more about how to execute a *production* than it is about spiritual *reproduction*.

Of course, productions in and of themselves are not necessarily the enemies of spiritual development. When we spend time and energy to produce excellent sermons, worship gatherings, children's ministries, discipleship classes and hospitality teams, we can certainly influence people's spiritual lives for good. We cannot deny the number of testimonies that have emerged from our Western style of doing church. But I would be remiss if I neglected to mention the danger lurking in the midst of all the activities and productions: namely the frequent lack of emphasis on *re*production and the charge of Jesus Christ to "go and make disciples."

Now, some may argue that Sunday celebrations or weekly church events accomplish just that, but in general, a Sunday celebration for most churches is much more about "come and see" than "go and make." I would submit that sometimes all of the work that goes into the production side of ministry can even serve as a type of spiritual narcotic. At times I have seen Christians get so excited about their service within the walls of the church that by the time it is all over, they just want to go home and rest. By the time they have finished the production of having church, they are too worn out to engage in the reproductive mission of God outside the church.

In recent years, churches have developed innovative ways to fill the airwaves with worship and the Word through live video streaming and social media outlets. Clearly, churches seem to do well in the air, but what about on the ground?

What if the internet network crashed or we could no longer use it? What would the Church's ground game look like? How would we continue to accelerate the mission of Christ if fewer people were committed to on-site church attendance?

Church growth expert George G. Hunter III laments, "The crisis of our time is that at least eight out of ten churches have not yet decided whether they intend to compete for the minds and hearts of human beings."[3] Many of these churches seem to experience a missional drift, and they do not even know it.

Now, this is certainly not to advocate that we stop our weekly gatherings at church buildings, because something powerful and effective transpires when the people of God gather together regularly. But what if God's intention is to grow nearer to people by means of an "everyday Church"? What would it be like if we started meeting in homes, coffee shops and even in our church buildings on a daily basis? What if gatherings of smaller numbers of people have the greater potential to make disciples? Or, to state it in a different way, what if God wants to see an everyday Church that is more relationally connected than collectively connected—more mission-driven than event-driven! What if the Supreme Commander and Chief of the Heavenly Hosts would prefer to change our ground game altogether to make it more reproduction-focused than production-focused?

"Go and Make" Christians

The word *go* involves continuous movement—go and keep on going and keep on going after that! According to this mandate, every Christ-follower should intentionally engage people with the purpose of introducing them to Christ. Jesus reinforced this idea, saying:

> "Go into all the world and preach the Good News to everyone."
>
> Mark 16:15 NLT

> "And as you go, preach, saying, 'The kingdom of heaven is at hand.'"
>
> Matthew 10:7

Recently, my wife, Kimberly, and I visited the site of the Alamo in San Antonio, Texas. The phrase "Remember the Alamo" speaks to the gallant bravery of a remnant of soldiers that included Davy Crockett and James Bowie, who fought against a powerful Mexican army led by General Santa Anna. Though the Mexican army prevailed at the Alamo, the significance of this battle inspired Sam Houston and his Texan forces to fight for a greater victory over Santa Anna just 46 days later, and their victory secured a much safer and liberated Texas in 1836.[4]

Despite the fact that "Remember the Alamo" became a rallying cry for victory, some historians believe that the deaths of those brave men were needless. Prior to the events of the Alamo, Commander Sam Houston had actually recommended a retreat and the destruction of the fort, but Colonel William Travis, who was responsible for the garrison, remained overconfident in his ability to defend his position. Bolstered by the resolute stance of his men, Travis made the fatal decision to stand firm and fight against overwhelming odds.[5]

Sadly, the form of Christianity I have started to describe above reminds me of the Alamo, as some Christians seem content with their fortress mentality. Whether consciously chosen or culturally conditioned, they have accepted the notion that their mere presence in a church building will ensure victory in the battle.

I would like to remind those Christians that we are not making a last stand at a church building! With church attendance steadily decreasing over the last decade, the Church at large faces overwhelming odds. The notion, "if we build it, they will come" is not a viable mantra anymore. Actually, if we build it, they will *not* come unless first we go out and bring them in.

When Jesus commissioned His disciples to "go into all the world and preach the gospel to every creature" (Mark 16:15), His word *world* (*kosmos* in Greek) was chosen to denote political systems or spheres of influence. In fact, the same word was used by the apostle Paul when he wrote that Satan was the "god of this *world*" (see 2 Corinthians 4:4). This implied that Satan does not seek to gain access to a physical location but rather to a sphere of influence. To the present day, as Satan continues to seek to infiltrate and manipulate this world's systems, we are called to proclaim the Gospel to the same.

Thankfully, Jesus' Great Commission to "go into all the world" does not mean that we have to move to the other side of the world to preach the Gospel; we have only to reach out to those in our own sphere of influence. To uproot our families and move to a foreign nation is not the highest goal, whereas sharing the Kingdom of heaven wherever we are is. Jesus instructed His disciples, "And as you go, preach, saying, 'The kingdom of heaven is at hand'" (Matthew 10:7).

So, what exactly does your closest mission field or sphere of influence look like? It can be your neighborhood or the marketplace, where all kinds of cultures already exist. Your closest mission field could be your community center, where leaders of all ages influence your city and neighborhood. In fact, you will find people of every color and creed, tribe and tongue in most population centers today.

I have decided to make my Uber driver my mission field. Oftentimes, an Uber trip gives me just enough time to direct a conversation toward an introduction to Christ. One morning I contacted an Uber driver for a ride to the airport, and I was able to share my faith with George (not his real name). Even though George had become an Uber driver to make some extra money, I found out that not long before this he had been involved in the hiring process of three thousand new employees for a prominent insurance company in the Dallas–Fort Worth area. Then of course, when the conversation eventually moved to what I do for a living, the door was wide open for me to talk about my religious beliefs.

George told me that his parents had divorced when he was young and that because of that, he had turned his back on religion and church attendance. Yet when he expressed his nominal belief in God's existence, I saw it as an opportunity to close his distance from God. I told George that he was more than flesh and blood and that he was a spiritual being who could find fulfillment only in the One who had created him. After a few minutes, he mentioned that I was the third person to talk with him about God over the past few weeks, and he half-jokingly admitted that these encounters must constitute some sort of a sign.

When we arrived at the airport and shook hands, I kept hold of his hand a few moments longer to pray with him that God might interrupt his life even more and begin a relationship with him. That exchange was a little unexpected, and I could tell that George was a bit shaken. But I knew that at the very least a seed had been planted in his heart.

When Jesus said, "Go into all the world [*kosmos*] and preach the Gospel to every creature," He issued a challenge to us to take the Gospel to our world or sphere of influence. But of course, Jesus also meant for us to take the Gospel to *all nations*. After all, that is how our initial passage from the Bible puts it,

"Go, therefore, and make disciples of all the nations" (Matthew 28:19). Here, "nations" (*ethnos* in Greek) refers specifically to ethnicities—to cultures, customs and civilizations. The implication is clear: Jesus' mandate to "go and make" urges Christians to engage every people group in every place! *Ethnos* (nation) refers to every people, and *kosmos* (world) refers to every place. God's heart reaches out to all people in all places.

Favorite Food for Christians

In the "come and see" approach to church, people often wait for others to come to them by means of some mysterious attraction, as if the fish will just jump into the boat without a pole or a net. Jesus counters this methodology, however; He teaches us to take up our nets and go fishing. He shows us how to do it, as He not only baits the hook and casts it into the water, but also shows us how to reel people into the Kingdom of God.

John's gospel tells the story of how Jesus encountered the Samaritan woman at the well, seeking her out to give her a transformative taste of eternal life. This is one of the most dramatic divine interruptions in the New Testament, in which Jesus purposefully sought out a sin-burdened woman who would never have sought Him out on her own (see John 4:4–26). On this occasion, Jesus exemplified the Great Commission even though He had not yet spoken about it to His disciples.

They had gone into the town to buy some food, and when they returned they were amazed to find Jesus in conversation with this woman:

> Just then his disciples came back. They were shocked to find him talking to a woman, but *none of them had the nerve to ask,* "What do you want with her?" or "Why are you talking to her?"
>
> John 4:27 NLT, emphasis added

Their questions are completely rational in light of the ancient context. Due to racial and religious rivalry, Jews and Samaritans had become alienated from each other. In fact, if anything, Jews like Jesus were expected to persecute Samaritans. Additionally, men did not usually interact with women in public, as women were viewed as second-class citizens in that day. Jesus' conversation with this particular woman exhibited a flagrant disregard for societal norms, all the more so because she turned out to be a notorious adulteress who had gone through five husbands.

On every level, this woman's life was shrouded by shame. This helps explain her decision to visit the well a half mile outside of town in the middle of the day; she did it in an effort to save herself from interaction with the other townspeople and potential embarrassment and ridicule. In the minds of the disciples, no decent man, let alone a rabbi or teacher, would have allowed himself to be seen in her company.

Nevertheless, the holiest man in the universe had stopped to share the truth of salvation with her.

What Do You Want with Her?

Just then his disciples came back. They were shocked to find him talking to a woman, but none of them had the nerve to ask, "What do you want with her?" or "Why are you talking to her?"

John 4:27 NLT

Their first question, "What do You want with her?" is the same as "What is the goal here?" The disciples did not understand why Jesus was engaged in a conversation with such a woman. The goal of their just-completed trip into the town had been to obtain food for the group. They were hungry, and they knew that He was, too. So now why waste time talking to someone like her?

But Jesus declined their offer of food. His conversation with the Samaritan woman had a greater purpose. For Jesus, unlike His disciples, the woman's eternal destiny assumed a much higher priority than His personal comfort.

In fact, their question, "What do You want with her?" was too important not to ask because His purpose was quite clear—to introduce her to Himself and to close her spiritual distance with God. As the New Testament Scripture illuminates:

> How can they call on him to save them unless they believe in him? And how can they believe in him if they have never heard about him? And how can they hear about him unless someone tells them?
>
> Romans 10:14 NLT

How many of us are like the disciples—we tend to think more about the moment (and our comfort) than about the eternal destiny of the people around us? So many of our decisions revolve around the maintenance of our personal comfort zone. I certainly recognize such a tension in my own life.

Not long ago on my return trip from a ministry visit to Africa, I ended up seated right next to a lovely Muslim woman. She was dressed in the traditional burka, and her hands and wrists were decorated with what I perceived to be a type of beautiful calligraphy. Although I did notice this, my primary desire was to sleep. After several days of teaching leaders in Nairobi, Kenya, I was wiped out and just wanted to rest.

But as we lifted from the runway, I began to notice that this woman kept clicking a small device that looked like a stopwatch. After we exchanged initial conversational pleasantries, I learned that the artistic designs on her hands and fingers exemplified a traditional art form; a dye called henna had been applied and, according to her, it represented an inner desire for elegance.

As we became more acquainted, I finally asked about the clicking instrument in her hand. She opened her hand to show me a device similar to a baseball pitch counter with the number 1,301 displayed on the face. She told me that she had asked Allah to forgive her 1,301 times so far during the flight. On the outside, I tried not to display my utter amazement, but on the inside, I was doing somersaults, especially when she said that all those clicks had taken place over a thirty-minute segment of time. Of course, this surprising discovery opened the door for a conversation about how Jesus Christ had died on the cross to forgive the sins of humankind once and for all.

Even though this precious woman did not make a decision to follow Christ after our conversation that day, I was glad I had not surrendered to my personal desire for the comfort of sleep. If I had, I would have missed this encounter with my own Samaritan woman. A consideration of the eternal destiny of this woman had superseded my wish for personal comfort.

Why Are You Talking with Her?

The disciples' first question really pointed to purpose while their second question related to motivation: "Why are You talking with her?"

Why, indeed? Why do you and I engage in evangelism? Do you ever feel guilty or ashamed because you have not introduced anyone to Christ lately? Or, do you end up on the other side of the spectrum with too much desire to impress others by your witness? Both of those motives fail to represent the Lord's desires.

For the longest time I felt that if I was not the one who prayed with someone to accept Christ, I had failed Him. But my real failure involved understanding the biblical principle that God does the saving and not me. When we overcome the effort to reach others on our own strength, we can cast aside our regrets and sense of failure. Always remember that you and I cannot save anyone—only He can.

And we are not solo players. Remember what Jesus said: "For in this the saying is true: 'One sows and another reaps.' I sent you to reap that for which you have not labored; others have labored, and you have entered into their labors" (John 4:37–38). My role is to sow the seed of the Good News, and if I happen to lead someone into a supernatural, born-again moment, I should realize that most likely I have just reaped the benefit of seed that was already sown by someone else.

This can be illustrated through a tool developed by James Engel, which shows a scale of eight steps that a nonreligious person might take toward salvation. Each step represents a specific connection point for Christians as they sow spiritual seeds in the life of a non-Christian.

Engel Scale

-8 Awareness of supreme being, no knowledge of the Gospel

-7 Initial awareness of Gospel

-6 Awareness of fundamentals of Gospel

-5 Grasp implications of Gospel

-4 Positive attitude toward Gospel

-3 Personal problem recognition

-2 Decision to act

-1 Repentance and faith in Christ

New Birth[6]

When you "go and make disciples," you may not necessarily have the opportunity to lead someone through the sinner's prayer, but most often you do have the unique privilege of moving an unbeliever toward the next step of his or her spiritual journey. Sometimes you may inspire the unbeliever to move toward awareness of the fundamentals of the Gospel (step six), while at other times, you may have the privilege of directing the person toward a decision to act (step two). For the most part, evangelism and discipleship involve simply moving people one step closer to God; their position relative to the Engel Scale is known only to God. I am sure that God's expectation and mission for each of us as Christ-followers is not to wrestle everyone we meet into the Kingdom, but humbly to sow seeds of the Gospel message.

Even when we grasp this truth, however, too many of us struggle with sharing Christ, more out of a lack of priority than a lack of desire. Truly our greatest ability lies in our availability, and that entails discernment of the appropriate times to engage with people. When your groceries are piled up on the checkout belt at the grocery store and the cashier cannot process your credit card payment, that may not be the best time to engage someone in a conversation about his or her eternal destiny. I have always believed that we must earn the right to be heard, especially when we speak to strangers about eternal issues.

With this in mind, we would do well to recognize that we will find it difficult to win a soul without a goal. Take notice of Jesus' response when His disciples offered Him the food they had brought; it becomes apparent that He had something else in mind:

In the meantime His disciples urged Him, saying, "Rabbi, eat."

But He said to them, "I have food to eat of which you do not know."

Therefore, the disciples said to one another, "Has anyone brought Him anything to eat?" Jesus said to them, "My food is to do the will of Him who sent Me, and to finish His work."

John 4:31–34

What is *your* favorite food? To surrender to God's will and to help finish His mission on earth? Do you relish going out of your way to encounter people like the woman of Samaria? Or do you tend to make a priority of your personal comfort and convenience? If you lean toward the latter, perhaps a recalibration of your priority list is in order. You and I have been summoned and commissioned to an all-important assignment. Success will be measured more by our unseen motives than by our spectacular results. I, for one, want to grow in my ability to filter the way I live my life through the grid of eternal destiny rather than personal comfort. Daily, I want to be on the lookout for my own Samaritan woman.

At the very least, a healthy tension should exist that challenges us to travel "through Samaria" when others might not do so. We must be willing to ask ourselves those hard-to-answer questions such as, "What do you want with her?" and "Why are you talking to her?" in order to ensure that our purpose and motives remain pure. In addition, we will need to keep reevaluating what sits at the top of our priority list. Truly, our food is to do the will of Him who sent us.

"Breathing" Christians

Have you ever watched the end of a marathon as runners stagger across the finish line with their ribs heaving and their heads bobbing like roosters? The extreme efforts of these runners to breathe come from their desperation. After a long and strenuous race, their life itself depends upon their ability to gulp in enough vital oxygen.

It goes without saying that everyone who lives also breathes. God created our physical bodies to breathe in and breathe out, inhale and exhale, many times a minute, day and night. In fact, on an ordinary day the average person's lungs pump enough air to fill a medium-size room or blow up several thousand party balloons.[7] Each breath sucks in a pint of air, and even without thinking about it, we take in around fifteen breaths per minute. Even the slightest change, such as when we climb the stairs or run to the car, can double our intake frequency.[8] Astoundingly, the entire process must continue while we are asleep, uninterrupted and without our conscious control, or else we would die. In reality, each one of us is really only five minutes from death![9] What a scary thought!

When God created the first man, He took a lump of clay and began to breathe into it, and then the thing that He created looked back at Him and returned the favor. As we inhale and exhale, we live, and if only one part of the process ceases to function, we die.

In much the same way, we inhale and exhale as we live out our faith, and if only one part of the process quits working, we move toward spiritual death. How many Christians attend church and experience the blessing of inhalation—hearing the Word and fellowshipping with the saints—but they do not engage in the blessing of exhalation—sharing the Word and reaching non-Christians? Perhaps it could be said that certain churches are dying because they are not breathing properly. They may breathe in with a "come and see" invitation, but they refuse to breathe out with a "go and make" mission.

Recently, I heard a representative from Global Outreach disclose this statistic: In their lifetime, 93 percent of Christians never share their faith with anyone else. Can this be true? That means that, almost unimaginably, when 93 percent of all Christians graduate to heaven, they will not take anyone with them. In other words, 93 percent of all Christians rest on their "blessed assurance" without even making an attempt to depopulate hell; 93 percent of Christians are more interested in sharing about Fox News or CNN than sharing the Good News of Jesus Christ.

No wonder some people and churches remain on life support! I just want to scream at the top of my lungs, "Breathe, for God's sake! Breathe and you will live! Breathe and your family will live! Breathe and the church will live! Breathe!" When I encounter people like this, I almost want to grab them and perform the Heimlich maneuver just to dislodge whatever obstacle has lodged itself inside them to inhibit their life in Christ.

When Martin Luther catalyzed the priesthood of all believers, all Christians were enlisted to serve as a grassroots movement to expand the Kingdom of God. The paradigm focus shifted from a Kingdom *with* priests to a Kingdom *of* priests. The weight of Kingdom expansion no longer rested on a select few but on masses of the chosen in every sector of society. Every Christian was appointed as a priest to his or her world. Every believer was to become a representative of Christ. As a result, the Kingdom expanded exponentially, because its growth was propelled from the bottom up and not the top down.

As we view the ecclesiastical landscape of the 21st century, the greatest challenge before the Church today is not socialism, communism, atheism or materialism. It is not even the advancement of Islam or certain social issues. No, the greatest challenge before the Church today is silent Christians. When it comes to sharing our faith, we must not "plead the Fifth."

What would happen if Christians would just breathe? What if we decided to share Christ as often as once a week? What would it look like if Christians would get off of their spiritual ventilators and share their faith with others? For those exhausted non-Christians whose race of life renders them victims of extreme oxygen deprivation, the Good News would become Great News.

Reproductive Christians

The stages of the reproductive process that takes place within a mother are astoundingly intricate. Even with all of our scientific understanding, we fail to comprehend everything our Divine Designer has conceived. Take the placenta, for instance. We know that it becomes enmeshed with the tissues of the mother, and that it creates a web of vessels with membranes so fine that all the chemicals in the mother's blood can enter into a child while all the waste products from the child can be diffused through the mother's circulation.[10] For months, cells pile on top of cells, and the uterine wall grows to one hundred times its resting size.[11] Finally at about the nine month mark, the uterine muscles, which have been gently contracting in waves throughout the mother's pregnancy, speed up dramatically, and the newborn child is pushed through the birth canal. Over an often-grueling nine month period, the woman's body has reordered its priorities toward the creation of a new life and not just the preservation of its own, familiar one.

Consider the similarities of childbirth to spiritual birth, the remarkable moment when the Divine Designer initiates rebirth in the spirit of a person. Jesus told Nicodemus, who earnestly sought the Kingdom of God:

> "Most assuredly, I say to you, unless one is born again, he cannot see the kingdom of God." Nicodemus said to Him, "How can a man be born when he is old? Can he enter a second time into his mother's womb and be born?"
>
> Jesus answered, "Most assuredly, I say to you, unless one is born of water and the Spirit, he cannot enter the kingdom of God."
>
> John 3:3–5

Here Jesus reinforced the importance of a spiritual *birth* in the Spirit, which signifies a new life and not merely a preservation of an old life.

Unbelievers find themselves persistently drawn to a supernatural moment when the contractions of the Holy Spirit shift them dramatically to a point of new birth. Through His death on the cross, Jesus has already prepared the way by becoming a type of spiritual placenta—His blood cleanses every sin and diffuses every impurity out of our spirits. Then at the appointed time, the unbeliever becomes a believer—almost immediately crying out as if to say, "I am alive!"

> If you confess with your mouth the Lord Jesus and believe in your heart that God has raised Him from the dead, you will be saved. For with the heart one believes unto righteousness, and with the mouth confession is made unto salvation.
>
> Romans 10:9–10

For everyone involved, including family and friends, nothing compares to this joyous occasion. Truly "reproductive" Christians experience the joy of this miracle time and again.

Sadly, some Christians fall far short where spiritual reproduction is concerned. A graphic example can be found in the biblical story of a woman named Tamar:

> Then Judah took a wife for Er his firstborn, and her name *was* Tamar. But Er, Judah's firstborn, was wicked in the sight of the Lord, and the Lord killed him. And Judah said to Onan, "Go in to your brother's wife and marry her, and raise up an heir to your brother." But Onan knew that the heir would not be his; and it came to pass, when he went in to his brother's wife, that he emitted on the ground, lest he should give an heir to his brother. And the thing which he did displeased the Lord; therefore He killed him also.
>
> Genesis 38:6–10

156

In this particular event, Tamar had married Judah's son Er, a wicked man who died before he could produce a child and heir. As was the custom at the time, Er's brother Onan assumed the responsibility of marrying Tamar in order to produce an heir. However, he did not want to produce an heir for his brother. He slept with Tamar, but he refused to engage in the reproductive process and instead spilled his semen on the ground. God's displeasure was clear and poignant: "I did not give this woman to you just to stimulate her, but to reproduce life within her." So, God killed him because he had failed to fulfill his purpose, which was to reproduce.

If we superimpose this spiritual principle on the Church today, we can see that God did not place His Church on this planet to spend all its time in stimulation. If His goal was merely for Christians to attend church services and have fellowship with the other saints, it would not matter if they fell short in the reproduction process and squandered God's seed. But that is not what He desires. To put it in the most basic terms, God did not marry His bride for stimulation but, significantly, for reproduction. Stimulation or excitement may be a part of the process, but that is not the purpose of it.

Christians have not been challenged merely to close the distance between themselves and God personally, but also to turn and help others do the same. In one of His more telling charges, Jesus declared: "By this My Father is glorified, that you *bear much fruit*; so you will be My disciples" (John 15:8, emphasis added).

Notice the specific call to "bear" much fruit. As His disciples, Christians have been commanded unequivocally to bear or reproduce fruit. In confirmation of this, Jesus continued:

"You did not choose Me, but I chose you and appointed you that you should *go and bear fruit*, and that your fruit should remain, that whatever you ask the Father in My name He may give you."

John 15:16, emphasis added

Do you see it? The link between "going and making disciples" and "going and bearing fruit" remains clear. We have been called to live as reproductive Christians.

One day I was on a run through my neighborhood when I happened upon a nail in the street. Without even thinking, I stopped and picked it up; I did not want anyone to step on it and get hurt or any car to drive over it and puncture a tire. As I held the nail in my hand and continued to run, the Lord inspired me to exhort others to "stop and pick up the nail."

What does that mean? Well, how often do we run across people who are sharp and cutting? These people could possibly harm others, and yet we turn away from them. Essentially, the nail I found in the street existed without a purpose; it was no longer connecting the frame of a house or the planks of a deck. It was not even in a container with other nails. It was lost and alone, without purpose. This situation needed to be remedied, so I stopped to pick up the nail.

Earl Creps, a prophetic church leader who continues to challenge existing church models, stated, "The key to the congregation's effectiveness is not unanimity or uniformity but mutual agreement on a common mission captured in the phrase 'Every soul matters to God.'"[12] Reproduction matters. A sense of purpose matters. Many churches and organizations have mission statements, but are they truly reproductive? As we evaluate ourselves, we should more often ask ourselves the question, "How many spiritual conversations have we experienced this week with unchurched people?" rather than "How many people attended our worship gathering this Sunday?" As reproductive

Christians, we are not just commissioned to create mission statements, but to go out and *live* them.

More than two billion people live on this planet who have not heard the message of Jesus Christ. Furthermore, the great revival and return of the Jewish people to the Messiah has not yet occurred; out of the 6.2 million Jews in Israel, there are only about 30,000 Messianic believers.[13] (That represents only about a half of one percent of the Jews in Israel.)

The harvest fields are ripe, and our mission is clear. Until Jesus Christ returns, the mandate to "go, therefore, and make disciples" will not change. We cannot ignore the charge to place reproduction over the production. After all, we call ourselves Christians, not "Churchians." So let's get up and get out there!

Personal CHALLENGE

In one of the more deeply moving books ever written, *The Insanity of God*, Nik Ripkin shares his personal pilgrimage about seeing God at work in the midst of persecution and martyrdom. First he shares many true stories from Somaliland, Russia, Ukraine, China, Southeast Asia and several Muslim-controlled nations, and then Ripkin summarizes his observations with this: "The greatest enemy of our faith today is not Communism, Buddhism, Hinduism, Atheism, or even Islam. Our greatest enemy is lostness."[14] His summary echoes Jesus' stated purpose, which was to "seek and save the lost" (Luke 19:10).

Ripkin observed that all over the world, believers choose to share Christ in Islamic, Hindu, Buddhist and Communist countries despite the potential for hostile consequences. The real issue for these Christians was not political freedom but obedience to Christ, and although the price of obedience might prove to be more costly in some places, sharing the message of Christ remained their highest priority.

Sadly, many of us in America do not choose to make the sharing of the Gospel our priority. Even though "persecution" for us may entail only mild mockery or rejection, we remain silent, which essentially means we choose to disobey the Great Commission. In fact, by remaining silent, we actually advance Satan's ultimate goal—to deny others the opportunity to draw near to God. In effect, we become accomplices with the enemy. Ripkin was once asked the question, "Is persecution coming to America?" and he retorted: "Why would Satan want to wake us up when he has already shut us up?"[15]

After I read Ripken's observations, I started asking myself a question in the morning, "Will I advance the call of Christ to 'go and make disciples' today, or will I live as an accomplice to Satan and remain silent?" Right now, ask yourself the same question: "Will I side with Jesus or with Satan today?" I remember what Ripkin's friend Stoyan, who had been persecuted for many years, reminded him: "Don't you ever give up in freedom what we would never give up in persecution."[16]

Personal EVALUATION

Right before the Lord Jesus Christ ascended to heaven, He issued some last-minute instructions to His disciples. In the words of the Great Commission, one of the most intense imperatives in the Bible, we catch a glimpse of God's global plan on earth and our role in it: "Go, therefore, and make disciples" (Matthew 28:19).

1. What does Jesus' charge to "Go, therefore, and make disciples" mean to you?

2. Reflect on the difference between *production* and *reproduction* in the Church. Which one should be the most important, and what are the implications for you?

3. How does the biblical principle "God does the saving and not me" impact your perspective about sharing Christ?

4. What obstacles do you encounter when you share about Christ? How can you overcome them?

5. Today, how will you choose to engage in God's global plan of reproduction?

Personal PRAYER

Heavenly Father, I hear Your charge to "go and make disciples," and I am renewing my commitment to participate actively in Your mission here on earth. I recognize that I have an important role to play in the eternal destiny of others. I am available to share my faith, and I accept my responsibility to live as more of a "go and make" Christian than a "come and see" Christian. Help me to inhale and exhale the life of the Spirit and live as a reproductive Christian, in Jesus' name. Amen.

Group CHALLENGE

Oftentimes we refer to "church" with reference to a location. We point to the corner of Interstate 25 and Highway 156 or mention the best-known spot near the church building. Naturally, churches are known for gathering at a certain location each week, but ultimately, the Church is not a building or a steeple or a place. The Church is a people, and people are everywhere.

Right before the Lord Jesus Christ ascended to heaven, He provided a glimpse of God's global plan on earth and our role in it: "Go, therefore, and make disciples" (Matthew 28:19). Allow the lessons you have learned in this chapter to guide you into a candid discussion concerning the mission of God's people on earth.

1. What does Jesus' charge to "Go, therefore, and make disciples" mean to you and to the Church?
2. Reflect on the difference between production and reproduction in the Church. Which one should be the most important, and what are some of its implications?
3. How does this one biblical principle, "God does the saving and not me," alter your perspective about sharing Christ?
4. Discuss the Engel Scale and how it can help you share the love of Christ more effectively.

Engel Scale

-8 Awareness of supreme being, no knowledge of the Gospel

-7 Initial awareness of Gospel

-6 Awareness of fundamentals of Gospel

-5 Grasp implications of Gospel

-4 Positive attitude toward Gospel

-3 Personal problem recognition

-2 Decision to act

-1 Repentance and faith in Christ

New Birth[17]

5. What obstacles do you encounter when you share about Christ? How can you overcome them?

6. If it is true that 93 percent of Christians never share their faith in their lifetime, discuss the implications of this statistic along with the notion that all believers are "priests" in the Kingdom of God.

7. Discuss Earl Creps' statement: "The key to the congregation's effectiveness is not unanimity or uniformity but mutual agreement on a common mission captured in the phrase 'Every soul matters to God.'"[18] Discuss how this should impact not only your daily life but also the eternal destiny of others.

9

Reflect Your Inner Jesus

"This sickness is not unto death, but for the glory of God, that the Son of God may be glorified through it."

John 11:4

As we all know, social media and the front-facing camera changed the course of history. Explore Instagram for sixty seconds, and you will find a plethora of selfies—Carmen with her pumpkin-spiced latte, Brian soaking up some sun at his favorite beach spot, candids of moms and dads with their beloved children.

In the course of the Democratic primary campaign of 2020, one of the candidates, Elizabeth Warren, touted the fact that she had taken over 100,000 selfies on the campaign trail. Actually, after one of her stump speeches in Manhattan, she had created a selfie line and spent four hours taking selfies with potential voters. She tweeted, "I don't spend my time asking rich donors for big checks—I spend it with voters. Our selfie line gives me a moment (or 100,000) to meet our movement."[1]

Now, there is certainly nothing wrong with an innocent selfie, and one may even applaud Warren's attempt to galvanize hopeful voters, but I wonder if the nature of the selfie underscores a deeper spiritual issue within our culture. Politics aside, what if the "Warren selfies" and the like betray a misplaced hope in the value of reflecting a certain image?

As you begin to draw nearer to God, your desires change; you begin to want to reflect your inner Jesus more and your inner self less. In your pursuit of His presence, a personal passion emerges—to glorify the Lord in all circumstances.

Of course, the circumstances do not always look as if they give glory to God. Take the story of Lazarus, for example (see John 11). When Jesus finally arrived at Bethany in response to an urgent summons, Lazarus had already been in the tomb for four days. It seemed to be too late, and both of Lazarus' sisters, Martha and Mary, cried out to Him, "Lord, if You had been here, my brother would not have died" (verses 21 and 32). They did not realize that Jesus had already hinted that this apparent tragedy had a greater purpose. He had told His disciples, "This sickness is not unto death, but for the glory of God, that *the Son of God may be glorified through it*" (John 11:4, emphasis added). In other words, Lazarus' untimely death would turn out to bring great glory to His Father and Himself.

Martha and Mary saw their brother's death as a permanent problem, while Jesus treated it as a temporary one. Sometimes, even when we truly seek to draw closer to God, we can allow temporary situations to discourage us from seeing the bigger picture. The storm seems to prevail until Jesus says, "Peace be still!" (see Mark 4:39). The paralysis seems to be permanent until Jesus says, "Arise and walk" (see Matthew 9:5). The tomb seems to be sealed for good until Jesus says, "Lazarus, come forth." The enemy of your soul looks for opportunities to take circumstances from the middle of your life and make them seem like they mark the end. I sometimes put it like this: Satan loves to mask your middle as the end.

You may think you are at the end of your rope, but if you are in Christ you are only in the middle. You may think you have done all you can and yet your marriage is still on the brink of collapse, but if you are in Christ you are just in the middle. You may think you have nothing of value left on this earth, and yet you are still in the middle of your story. What the enemy likes to convince you is the end, the Lord still calls the middle or even a new beginning in the middle.

Amazingly, as Lazarus and his sisters discovered, even the grave is only the middle. Even death is not the end! Because Jesus Christ is the Resurrection and the Life, death is only temporary. Of course death seems sorrowful and insufferable and dark. A stone may seem to block the way out, and the grave may mark the end of an earthly life—but as we see in this story, it is still in the middle. The end of earthly life, for those who belong to God, is the beginning of eternal life.

Remember: Your middle is not your tomb; it is your womb. Your middle is not a messed-up moment; it is a blessed-up moment. As the familiar words of the Twenty-Third Psalm declare:

> Yea, though I walk through the valley of the shadow of death, I will fear no evil; for You are with me; Your rod and Your staff, they comfort me. . . . Surely goodness and mercy shall follow me all the days of my life; and I will dwell in the house of the LORD forever.
>
> Psalm 23:4, 6

Yes, at any moment, physical death may take you by the hand. But in the process, it gloriously transitions you to a new and eternal dwelling place with God.

In the case of Lazarus, however, Jesus chose to raise him from death back to earthly life, and this brought great glory to God. It is interesting to note that both Mary and Martha, who were grief-stricken and even upset with Jesus when He showed up too late, were easily able to glorify Him *after* their brother's miraculous resurrection.

Most of us find it quite difficult, if not impossible, to choose to give glory to God in the midst of the struggle and not just in the final victory. Over time, however, we can live more and more in confident faith. Because His Spirit dwells in us, we can learn how to intentionally reflect our inner Jesus in every circumstance, no matter how tough. And we will find that "the Son of God may be glorified through it."

Reject Your Inner Judas

You and I can understand why Martha and Mary questioned the Lord's belated arrival. Sometimes we can feel let down or betrayed by Him at critical moments. In some cases, our feelings can even cause us to betray Him. That is when another voice can be heard—the voice of Judas.

As we know, Judas Iscariot was the disciple who would eventually betray Jesus with a kiss. That was not the first time he had acted as an antagonist. Once at a meal in Bethany (some time before Lazarus fell ill and died), Judas had voiced his disapproval. Do you remember the account of how Mary lavished an expensive ointment on Jesus' feet and wiped them with her hair? As Jesus conversed with Lazarus at the table and Martha waited on her guests, Mary decided to go to extraordinary lengths to show glory to the Lord, while Judas had other plans.

One of His disciples, Judas Iscariot, Simon's son, who would betray Him, said, "Why was this fragrant oil not sold for three hundred denarii and given to the poor?" This he said, not that he cared for the poor, but because he was a thief, and had the money box; and he used to take what was put in it.

John 12:4–6

Betrayal of Intimacy

This was a different kind of betrayal—a betrayal of intimacy. By his remarks, Judas had attempted to sabotage Mary's expression of love and gratitude. Although he raised an objection that seemed reasonable, he probably also felt uncomfortable to see such an intimate act. Like most orthodox Jews, he would have considered a woman's hair to be erotic, and he would have felt that it should remain covered except in front of her husband or in the company of other women. By letting down her hair in such an immodest way, she disregarded her exposure to reproach for the sake of expressing her heartfelt devotion on Jesus.

Yet Mary's moment of intimacy with Jesus was so important that John ended up mentioning her expression of generosity even before he told the account of Lazarus' resurrection. When he did so, John elevated the status of her action, and he made it almost equivalent to or even greater than the magnificence of Lazarus' miracle:

Now a certain man was sick, Lazarus of Bethany, the town of Mary and her sister Martha. It was that Mary who anointed the Lord with fragrant oil and wiped His feet with her hair, whose brother Lazarus was sick.

John 11:1–2

Just as Judas spoke out against Mary in an attempt to betray her selfless act of intimacy with Jesus, so your "inner Judas" loves to speak up whenever you begin to draw near to Him. Your inner Judas relentlessly seeks to create obstacles to distract you from finding that intimate moment with Him: "What are you doing? You really do not have time for this. Your schedule is too busy. You need to spend your time and treasure on something else rather than this."

Mary wanted to give all she had to Jesus, but Judas was concerned with material gain more than with spending time with Jesus. Mary was extravagant and unconditional in her love; Judas was limited and conditional. Mary wanted to spend everything on Jesus, while Judas implied he wanted to spend the cost of the ointment on others.

Sadly, your inner Judas sees things differently from your inner Jesus. Your inner Judas prowls around looking for ways to steal from you. Your inner Judas seeks to control the money box and steal your intimacy with the Lord. Only if you love the Lord your God with your heart, mind, soul and strength will you be able to reject your inner Judas and disregard the enemy's attempt to sabotage your intimacy with God.

Betrayal of Generosity

Mary's act of intimacy was more generous than it might seem. The pound of ointment would have cost the equivalent of about a year's wages. Think about your own annual income for a moment. Regardless of how high or low it is, it is your entire income for a whole year. Now imagine giving it all away in a few minutes. Judas could not fathom it. If I were to paraphrase his comment, it might sound something like this: "Why would you pour a year's wages on Jesus' feet of all places? Why did you not just wash His feet with water? And why did you dry His feet with your hair instead of a towel?"

Your inner Judas loves to betray your generosity as well as your intimacy.

Think about your hands. Even now as you read, just take a quick look at them. When you were just an infant, you would grasp your mother's little finger tightly and not let go. As you grew, you grabbed rattles and little toys. And when another child would try to take them away from you, you would snap, "Mine!" and hold on tight.

Later, when you were in junior high school, you held on tightly to bicycle handlebars and batons and instruments. In high school, you hung on to the hand of your friends. In college, you may have held on to some stuff you probably should not have, but when you left, hopefully you clutched a diploma with both hands. When you started a career, you grabbed on to the lowest rung of the ladder, and since then, you have been climbing as fast as you can. Someday retirement will come, and you will hang on to golf clubs and gardening tools and pension funds and Social Security checks. Eventually, as the years pass by, you may need to clutch canes and walkers and eventually hospital beds and life itself.

By human nature, we are "clutchers." We scrape and claw and work and fret, and if we get ahead even a little bit, we hold on with all our might to whatever we have acquired. Even when Jesus' Spirit within us encourages us to relax our grip, our inner Judas tries to control the money box and derail our generosity.

Sadly, though, closed hands do not help to close the distance between us and God. All throughout history and Scripture, God models what it means to have open hands by generously providing food, shelter, clothing, protection and blessing. The psalmist declared: "You open Your hand and satisfy the desire of every living thing" (Psalm 145:16).

When Jesus walked the earth, He showed us how to be generous in every way. He did not live His life with closed hands. He did not clutch His possessions. He did not refuse to give His

171

love, healing and resources to those who were in need. He did not shake a clenched fist at those who flogged Him and nailed Him to the cross. He lived and continues to live with open, generous hands.

While He was on earth, Jesus continually healed the sick, touched the people in pain and blessed those who were in despair. He gave His love, His heart, His time and His treasure. And when He was asked to give up the only thing He had left, His very life, He stretched His arms out and opened up His hands of generosity so that steel spikes could be driven into them.

Once and for all, He showed us how to reject our inner Judas and embrace a new way of life. Now, because of Him, we are free to walk through our lives generously, even to the point of death, with a new heart and a heavenly perspective.

Never forget the end of the narrative with regard to Mary's extravagant love. We read this statement of legacy in Mark's account. In Jesus' own words, "Assuredly, I say to you, wherever this gospel is preached in the whole world, what this woman [Mary] has done will also be told as a memorial to her" (Mark 14:9).

After approximately two thousand years, we still read about the generosity of one ordinary woman who loved Jesus above all else. As for Judas, however, we read in the very next verses:

Then Judas Iscariot, one of the twelve, went to the chief priests to betray Him to them. And when they heard it, they were glad, and promised to give him money. So he sought how he might conveniently betray Him.

Mark 14:10–11

For two millennia, as the course of history has progressed with all of its twists and turns, Mary is known for her generosity while Judas is known for his betrayal. I am sure I do not have to tell you which example to follow.

Reflect Your Inner Jesus

When the container of oil is broken open and the ointment first touches Jesus' feet, its sweet-scented fragrance fills not only the room but every heart in every place where Jesus is adored, right through the generations to our own.

This is why, when we begin to draw nearer to God, our lives become a fragrance to others. As we move through our lives, we reflect something beyond ourselves and our own desires—we radiate the heart of Jesus, and everything else falls by the way-side. As John the Baptist declared, "He must increase, but I must decrease" (John 3:30).

And notice the result when we choose to do so—

His divine power has given to us *all things that pertain to life and godliness*, through the knowledge of Him who called us by glory and virtue, by which have been given to us exceedingly great and precious promises, that through these you may be partakers of the divine nature, having escaped the corruption that is in the world through lust.

2 Peter 1:3–4, emphasis added

All Things That Pertain to Life and Godliness

Our God provides us with "all things that pertain to life and godliness." In other words, we have not been destined for death or failure; there is a way that leads to life, and it has been made available to us!

We cannot deny we live in the midst of a performance-driven culture in which an inner Judas constantly berates us with the possibility of failure. He poses questions to our minds: "What if you fail as a parent? What if you fail in your career? What if you fail as a Christian?" Sometimes failure can seem like a five-hundred-pound gorilla in the room that never seems to go away. But despite the anxiety and fear caused by the beast of failure, we can learn to reflect upon God's promise that we have everything we need to succeed. Our "inner Jesus" frees us to depend upon what *He* can do rather than what we can do. He shows us the way; our potential is not dependent upon our ourselves but on Him.

Without a doubt, I can at times look foolish and do foolish things, but God is able to overcome even my own foolishness. I have decided to be thankful for the scriptural assertion: "But God hath chosen the foolish things of the world to confound the wise" (1 Corinthians 1:27 KJV). The word *foolish* comes from the Greek word *moraine*, from which we get our English word *moron*. When God chose me, He chose someone who can look and act like a moron at times.

One day, I went through a Wendy's drive-through, and I ordered a cheeseburger, French fries and a Frosty. Only as I pulled forward did I realize that I had been talking to the trash can instead of the speaker system. I am sure I looked like a moron. Or recently, I was on a road trip with someone, and we stopped at a gas station to use the restroom. When I walked out of the gas station, I opened the door of the truck only to realize I had started to climb into the wrong truck with a very startled person behind the wheel. Of course, the driver of the truck looked at me like I was a moron.

I am sure at some time or another, you have had similar experiences. And whether or not others are acting like morons, our world today teems with derisive people who find it easy to label others accordingly. But not so with God! God chooses the morons and idiots of this world to confound the wise. Even when we fail and make mistakes, God still chooses to use us. Even when we miss the mark and act foolish, God does not disqualify us. He reaches out to us and provides access through His divine power to "all things that pertain to life and godliness." Our weakness gives His glory a chance to shine.

Simply stated, this God of morons chooses our moronic moments, and He does it all the time, purely to call us into a greater depth of His glory and virtue. Remember the truth of 2 Peter 1:3—"His divine power has given to us all things that pertain to life and godliness, through the knowledge of Him who called us by glory and virtue."

Called by Glory and Virtue

Glory and virtue? For many of us, the biblical notion of "glory" remains ambiguous and nebulous. What does the term *glory* actually mean, particularly with reference to God? When we say, "Give God the glory" or "I glorify Your name," what exactly do we intend to say? In essence, the word *glory* (*doxa* in Greek) refers to "greatness." So when we give God glory, we provide a highlight reel of what He is famous for.

Athlete Lebron James is considered great because of his skills on the basketball court, so his fame—his glory—is specifically linked to his ability to play basketball. Similarly, Tiger Woods is famous for golf, and his glory is derived from his ability to strike the golf ball. What is God famous for?

We do not need to look far for the answer, because God answered the question Himself:

> Moses said, "Please. Let me see your Glory."
>
> GOD said, "I will make my Goodness pass right in front of you; I'll call out the name, GOD, right before you."
>
> Exodus 33:18–19 MESSAGE

In effect, God had announced to Moses, "I am famous for being good."

One of the most famous sermons of all time, delivered by the colonial theologian Jonathan Edwards in the eighteenth century, is titled, "Sinners in the Hands of an Angry God." A more accurate title perhaps should have been, "Sinners in the Hands of a Loving God." Because God is famous for His love and His goodness, we sinners do not glorify Him as an angry God but as a loving God.

Before Lazarus was raised from the dead, Jesus had already hinted that a greater purpose was in play here, as He had told His disciples, "This sickness is not unto death, but for the glory of God, that *the Son of God may be glorified through it.*"

Lazarus' sickness was a divine interruption. And Jesus would be glorified or made famous as a result of it. Certainly, on the surface, if we assume that Jesus only sought greater fame, a statement like this could seem self-serving. But ultimately, Jesus was not taking a personal selfie at all. He was simply reflecting the divine power of God, which happened to demonstrate in the process a power capable of overcoming death. As we find out later in the gospel narrative, Lazarus' resurrection also served as a harbinger of Jesus' own resurrection.

In such instances, God demonstrates His great resurrection power to prove His authority in our lives, and during those times, we can more easily reflect our inner Jesus. But what about those times when He does not perform an instantaneous miracle, or when we are still waiting? Can we glorify Him as Sovereign Lord even when He seems distant?

Some people misunderstand the sovereignty of God when they proclaim, "God can do *anything.*" Actually, there are things God cannot really do, since He cannot compromise the scope of His moral virtue. "Virtue" (*apete* in Greek) of course suggests moral excellence of character, which begs the question: Has God ever wanted to do something outside of His moral excellence of character?

In the book of Exodus, God wanted to eliminate the children of Israel from the face of the earth due to their wickedness. And yet, because He had made a covenant with them, His glory and virtue caused Him to relent. Other examples of what God will not do: He will not lie because His moral excellence will not allow for it, and He will not deceive because His goodness restrains Him from evil. In other words, even if He wanted to lie and deceive, the nature of His character prevents Him from doing so. We can rejoice that God's sovereignty is not based on what He can and cannot do; His sovereignty is founded on who He *is*.

What is even more magnificent, however, is that God has not reserved His nature only for Himself. As a Christian, you and I have access to His glory and virtue! The more you become like God, the more you are able to live in His glory (goodness) and virtue (moral excellence). At times, you may want to pinch someone's head off, but God's goodness and moral excellence will restrain you. You may want to harbor unforgiveness toward someone who has offended you, but God's goodness and moral excellence will convict you. You may want to live angry at everyone around you, but God's goodness and moral excellence will convince you otherwise.

This is your inner Jesus, which seeks to reflect His glory and virtue. And the result? "Exceedingly great and precious promises"!

His divine power has given to us all things that pertain to life and godliness, through the knowledge of Him who called us by glory and virtue, by which have been given to us *exceedingly great and precious promises*, that through these you may be partakers of the divine nature, having escaped the corruption that is in the world through lust.

2 Peter 1:3–4

As we reflect our inner Jesus, we receive God's promises, which are not just great and precious, but *exceedingly* great and precious.

His Exceedingly Great and Precious Promises

Has God ever made a promise to you? Have you ever known down in the inner recesses of your heart and mind that God's promise to you would come to pass? Perhaps He gave you a promise that your spouse or your children would be saved, or that you would build a business or receive a promotion. Or possibly He promised you that you would do missions work in a foreign country or serve in a great church. Because of God's glory and virtue, we now know that these promises will come to pass! After all, He is a keeper of His word.

Exceedingly Great Promises

The word *great* (*megistos* in Greek) actually means "very great" or "the greatest." Have you ever noticed that God usually does not provide small promises? His promises are very great or the greatest. His promises usually are not small because the problems in the way of those promises are never small.

Noah spent 120 years building an ark on dry land before it ever started raining. Literally, he built an ark in the dark, ignoring his friends who mocked him, saying, "This boat will never float."

David ran down a hill with only a slingshot and a rock to face a giant monstrosity of a man over nine feet tall, clad in over a hundred pounds of armor. Everyone else cowered in fear as David, almost unarmed, faced a giant's sword and spear.

Providentially, when the problem is great, the Promise-Maker is always greater. When everything seems to be collapsing around us, we can compare our problem to the Promise-

Maker, and we can remember who gave us the promise to begin with.

One day I listened to myself as I sang the words of a popular worship song to God: "You have no rival . . . no equal. . . . God, You reign."

But as I sang, I realized that I did not need to remind God that He reigned. He already knew it. Even though I had sung the words to God, what had really happened in my spirit was that I had reminded myself of God's sovereignty and authority. I had encouraged myself that God has no rival and no equal. Sometimes we simply need to reinforce the notion that we are His children, and He is bigger than our problem.

Even our own kids do not allow problems to hinder their promises. If I told my sons that I would buy them a baseball bat for the upcoming little league season, no problem would hinder that promise. If the sporting-goods store did not have the right sized bats in stock, it would not matter because Dad would find a way to keep his promise. And if we found a bat that was too costly, far outside our price range, Dad would still keep his promise. Of course, we would not take Mom on our shopping ventures because she would never understand why we would pay hundreds of dollars for a baseball bat. However, for my sons, the problem would never become bigger than the promise.

For Daddy God, the problems do not hinder the promises. If Daddy God promised it, He will fulfill His promise. All we need to remember is that He reigns, now and forever. The Kingdom and the glory belong to Him, and His exceedingly great promises will never be broken.

Exceedingly Precious Promises

The word *precious* (*timios* in Greek) denotes the idea of something valuable, costly or expensive. Are your promises too precious to let go of? Are your promises so precious or valuable that you will not give up on them? Quite likely the people who give up on their promises do not value them enough to hold on to them. When you consider your promise to be exceedingly precious, you will not be deterred by the size of your problem.

Like Noah, you will spend a hundred and twenty years to build an ark in the dark if it means the salvation of your family. Or like David, you will charge down the hill with a slingshot to defeat a giant because it means the salvation of your nation. Notice that David did not stay up on the mountain with the rest of the army; his promise was so precious that he descended into the valley to fight the giant. While it is true that problems arise in the valley, if you stay up on the mountaintop with everyone else, you will most likely miss the realization of your promise.

The precious nature of the promise should overcome the persistent effort of the problem. When you hold your promise as exceedingly valuable, you will not remain frustrated by the problem, but the problem will become frustrated by you. If your promise is precious, the hero in you will not be controlled by the human in you. Or, stated more simply, you will reject your inner Judas and reflect your inner Jesus.

As you cling to your promises and pursue the glorious virtue of God, there is a miraculous result: His divine nature will be reproduced within you!

As His divine power has given to us all things that pertain to life and godliness, through the knowledge of Him who called us by glory and virtue, by which have been given to us exceedingly great and precious promises, that *through these you may be partakers of the divine nature, having escaped the corruption that is in the world through lust.*

2 Peter 1:3–4, emphasis added

Partakers of the Divine Nature

God's promises are not given merely to bless us but also to produce godliness in us. In fact, increased godliness is one of His blessings. His promises enhance our ability to become more like Christ, and they help us take on His divine nature. In other words, His promises help us to look like Him and live like Him. The closer we get to our promises, the closer we get to God!

According to this Scripture and also from inescapable first-hand evidence—the signs of the times that we all can see—our world is corrupt. The word *corruption* (*phthora* in Greek) refers to deep moral deterioration. We discover that the closer we get to the world, the more we end up smelling like it.

One day I had worked in my backyard and had not noticed that I had stepped in some dog doo. I did not know about it until after I had tracked it all over the white carpet in our house and my wife smelled it and pointed it out to me. In much the same way, we can get so close to the world that we find the world's "doo" on our shoe, and we do not realize it until we have tracked it everywhere. Wherever we go, we leave a trail of the world's deep moral deterioration.

While the word *corruption* refers to deep moral deterioration, the word *lust* (*epithymia* in Greek) illustrates deep immoral desire. The Bible calls it the "lust of the flesh, the lust of the eye, and the pride of the life" (1 John 2:16). Just reflect on the dealings and affairs of political leaders and even community and church leaders over the last few years, and think how extensively the foul odor of deep immoral desire has been tracked into every sector of society.

Yet despite the tremendous stench we may find in the world, we will discover that as we draw nearer to God, we will also draw closer to His divine nature, and thus escape pervasive corruption and lust. We gladly exchange the moral deterioration and immoral desires that envelop this world for the nature or character of God.

To define and describe the word *character*, I like to say "character is the echo of your life." Just as sound echoes off walls, your character echoes off the walls of your life. Your character reflects how people think about you, remember you and even feel about you. Every aspect of your character will leave echoes in the hearts of the people you encounter. That is why it is so important to reflect your inner Jesus. When you tap into His divine character, you leave the echoes of God's divine nature in the hearts of others.

I believe that you can develop such a connection to the divine nature of God that you can emanate God's presence wherever you go. You can walk into a room and people will say, "That person reflects the presence of Christ." I have heard such comments after a particular person has walked into a church gathering. They may note, "As soon as I walked in, I felt something different. Then I cried through the entire service, and I don't know why." I know why: Such experiences happen when people are moved by the presence of God.

Granted, the theology of people who are content with emotionless Christianity or controlled spiritual experiences will be disturbed by statements like this. But God has granted us the liberty to choose whether or not we will open ourselves to His presence, and for the most part we can choose to diminish our awareness of His divine interruptions if we so desire.

Unfortunately, countless people walk through life aware only that God has stamped their ticket on the train to heaven. This means that they miss out on the joyous adventure with the Conductor and the other people along for the ride, as well as the personal transformation that occurs. When we become so infused with God's divine nature, we cannot help but reflect Him as we travel through the vicissitudes of daily life.

God offers both His omnipresence and His manifest presence. Omnipresence alludes to His existence everywhere at the same time. He is that "particle" in the atomic nucleus of everything that holds the universe together. If this world lacked God's presence for even a millisecond, it would cease to exist. But God offers even more than His omnipresence, since He sometimes chooses to concentrate or intensify His presence. For divine reasons that only He understands, He at times also chooses to reveal Himself in greater concentration right *here* more than over there, or right *now* instead of later on. In those times, God's omnipresence takes on the added dimension of His manifest presence.

When you begin to reflect your inner Jesus through His manifest presence, the people who know you best will say, "This one's been with Jesus. He used to be unlearned and ignorant. She used to be shy and reserved. He used to be angry and impatient. She used to be a problem child in a problem family. But now, I see Jesus."

As you will know if you have ever gone to a professional basketball game, the best seats in the house are in the front row. The VIPs and the big stars are invited to sit in the front row, where they are privileged to get closer to all the action. They can actually interact with the players on the court and hear the coaches strategize during timeouts. When we consider how to draw nearer to God, we need to remember that He does not want us to settle for the back row. We should make it our goal to get as close to all the action as possible.

When Elizabeth Warren worked her selfie line in Manhattan, she may have described herself as a candidate who wanted to capture snapshots of hopeful voters. But the source of all political hope remains fixed in human striving, not in the One who is the source of all true hope. All such human endeavors will wind up on social media for sixty seconds, only to fade into distant memory.

Our only hope remains in getting as close to the front row of His divine presence as possible. When we begin to do that, we will find it normal to reject our inner Judas and to reflect our inner Jesus. Sometimes, we will face times of struggle—Lazarus will die. Other times, we will experience moments of victory when he lives. But in every situation, we will honor Him as Mary did, and we will live so "that the Son of God may be glorified through it."

Personal CHALLENGE

In this personal challenge, take a look at your hands. Do you like what you see? Do they look like Mary's hands that love to pour the oil and wipe the feet of Jesus? Are they open and generous hands like the hands of Christ? Or, do you think instead of the way they tend to grasp and clutch?

I hope you like what you see and can appreciate what God has done in your life. But if you do not, you will be glad to know that you can change them; a change of hands will occur through a change of heart. If you will allow God to change your heart, then you will see a change of hands.

"But how do I know if God is changing my heart?" you may ask. You will know by what happens inside of you. If you frequently reject your inner Judas, then your heart is changing. And if you are glad to reflect your inner Jesus, then your heart is changing.

British missionary author C. T. Studd wrote, "Only one life, 'twill soon be past, only what's done for Christ will last."[2] Take the time right now to evaluate yourself through the following questions.

Personal EVALUATION

1. Whether Lazarus dies or lives, our challenge is to give glory to God. Evaluate your own passion to glorify the Lord in all circumstances.

2. When Mary washed Jesus' feet, Judas tried to betray her intimacy with Christ. What are some specific ways that your inner Judas seeks to betray your intimacy with Christ?

3. Mary is remembered for her generosity and faith while Judas is known for his greed and betrayal. Discuss the importance of modeling your life on Mary's.

4. Discuss some of the exceedingly great and precious promises that Christ has afforded you.

5. When you reflect your inner Jesus, you glorify Him in all circumstances. What are your current circumstances, and how can you bring glory to the Lord in the midst of them?

Personal PRAYER

Heavenly Father, I am passionate about giving glory to You and Your Son, Jesus Christ. Even though the circumstances around me seem permanent, I know that they are only temporary in Jesus' name. I choose to respond with gratitude and generosity. I will reject my inner Judas and reflect my inner Jesus. By Your divine power, I have access to all things that pertain to life and godliness. I will walk in Your glory and virtue, and through the exceedingly great and precious promises that You have provided, I will reflect Your divine nature, which will enable me to escape the corruption that is in the world through lust. I choose to glorify You in every circumstance. For Yours is the Kingdom, power and glory forever. Amen.

Group CHALLENGE

As you begin to draw nearer to God, you will desire to reflect your inner Jesus more than your inner Judas. A personal passion will emerge that looks for ways to glorify the Lord in all circumstances. What does this look like? Discuss as a group where you see yourself within the framework of this chapter.

1. Whether Lazarus dies or lives, our challenge is to give glory to God. Evaluate your own passion to glorify the Lord in all circumstances.

2. When Mary washed Jesus' feet, Judas tried to betray her intimacy with Christ. What are some specific ways that your inner Judas seeks to betray your intimacy with Christ?

3. Mary is remembered for her generosity and faith while Judas is known for his greed and betrayal. Discuss the importance of modeling your life on Mary's. What does a life of generosity and faith look like?

4. Discuss the verse: "But God hath chosen the foolish things of the world to confound the wise" (1 Corinthians 1:27 KJV). Share pertinent examples from your own experience.

5. Discuss your thoughts about laying hold of

   a. all things that pertain to life and godliness

   b. His divine glory and virtue

   c. His exceedingly great and precious promises

   d. His divine nature.

6. Discuss some of the exceedingly great and precious promises that Christ has afforded us as believers.

7. When we reflect our inner Jesus, we glorify Him in all circumstances. Share about the circumstances in your life right now and how you can bring glory to the Lord in the midst of them.

10

Cheering You on
to the End

"And be sure of this: I am with you always, even to
the end of the age."

Matthew 28:20 NLT

My daughter, Grace, ran track for a few years in junior
high school. Because she was lightning fast, she ran
the 100- and 200-meter sprints and the 4 x 100-meter
relay. I liked to watch her run track for just those few seconds
each race even though it meant I had to spend many hours
waiting between her events.

During that time, I saw quite a few races, and occasionally,
I would notice a young boy or girl who lagged far behind the
other racers in an event. In these instances, most parents would

just cheer their child on to finish the race, but every so often a parent would emerge from the stands without regard for the other people they had to step over, in order to yell at the top of his or her lungs, "C'mon! Run faster! Run faster!!" Usually the poor child would be struggling for breath, and the incredulous, exasperated look on his or her sweaty face would say it all: "I'm running as fast as I can!"

I would not be surprised if many of us have experienced something similar. Voices around us are always screaming, "C'mon! Go faster! Go faster! Be better! Work harder!" These voices may come from our parents, but more likely they come from other sources such as our bosses, our pastors, our spouses or, naturally, even from within ourselves. So with distressed faces and veins that protrude from our necks, we make every effort to comply. We strive to do our best while, ever-increasingly, we live our lives in the fast lane.

An unfortunate result of conducting our lives at such a dizzying speed is that we tend to leave God behind. Granted, we do not consciously reject Him; we just do not necessarily feel that we have time to include Him in our daily schedule. The late Michael Yaconelli wrote an inspiring book about the tensions of faith in which he suggests, "Christianity is not about inviting Jesus to speed through life with us; it's about noticing Jesus sitting at the rest stop."[1]

For years, I was told that I had not given God my best unless I had given 100 percent. Even though the premise was stated with sincerity and it sounded spiritual, all I knew was that I fell far short of 100 percent on many days. I might wake up with a high, 100-percent commitment level, but after I had trudged through life as usual for a few hours, that level of commitment would fall to 82 percent or even 65 percent. I could see that various life circumstances would help me at times, since my percentage would spike in celebratory moments such as the birth of a child or a promotion at work, and it would drop in times when I felt more fragile, such as when I suffered from sickness or a friend or family member passed away.

Speaking candidly, I watched this firsthand as my dad struggled against four different types of cancer for seventeen long years. His health problems drove down his ability to give God his best. I would say that his best percentage of commitment to God certainly fluxuated, especially near the end of his sickness. He remained highly committed to doing his best for God, but could never measure up to his high intentions; his best endeavors fell short because of his rigorous daily circumstances. Yet God did not fluctuate in His love for my dad, and He graciously received whatever he could offer to Him.

God loves all of us that way.

God Is Near and Never Far

The apostle Paul preached to the Athenian Greeks on Mars Hill after pointing to an altar with the inscription: "To the Unknown God." In his message, he proceeded to explain why and how the One True God does not have to remain unknown or far removed:

> Starting from scratch, He [God] made the entire human race and made the earth hospitable, with plenty of time and space for living so we could seek after God, and not just grope around in the dark but actually *find* him. He doesn't play hide-and-seek with us. He's not remote; he's *near*. We live and move in him, can't get away from him.
>
> Acts 17:26–28 Message

The idea of groping around in the dark makes me think of a time when I was a young adult and stayed at a house with a bedroom that did not have a light switch. Instead, it had a single light bulb in the middle of the room, and I could turn it on only with a pull string. Because there was no switch conveniently located by the door, I always had to enter the room in complete darkness and begin waving my hands in all directions in an effort to find what seemed to be the invisible pull string. One time I hit my shin on a coffee table in the middle of the room and cried out with pain as I hopped around on one leg. (A video of that episode would have been funny enough for *America's Funniest Home Videos*.)

Sadly, when it comes to our search for God, some people believe that it is a prerequisite to grope around in the dark, and that they must hit their shins on unexpected suffering before they can find Him. They feel that if only they can somehow flail around until they find the invisible string that flips the light on, then they will be allowed to see God and all His glory.

But hide-and-seek is unnecessary with God. He is near and never remote. In fact, we cannot really get away from Him because He makes Himself known in the way we live and move and have our being.

Just as God interrupted Adam and Eve's game of hide-and-seek in the bushes, He seeks to do the same with us. He has opened the way to divine relationship and intimacy by sending His Son, Jesus Christ, so that the people who meet Him can begin to get acquainted with God Himself. When the time came for Jesus to ascend to heaven, God sent His Spirit to remain ever-present with those who believe, near and dear always. From that time forward, God has remained with us at all times, fulfilling His promise to be with us "always, even to the end of the age" (Matthew 28:20).

And take careful note: God has prepared one final divine interruption for the future, and He wants us to be ready for it:

> For the Lord himself will come down from heaven with a commanding shout, with the voice of the archangel, and with the

trumpet call of God. First, the believers who have died will rise from their graves. Then, together with them, we who are still alive and remain on the earth will be caught up in the clouds to meet the Lord in the air. Then we will be with the Lord forever.

1 Thessalonians 4:16–17 NLT

As we look at the 21st century, we are dreadfully aware of the uncertainty before us. More and more, chaotic circumstances, whether human-made or naturally induced, arise and challenge us to "mind our gaptivity" with God. Our answer will always and only be found if we run toward Him and not away from Him. Those who know Him will find Him to be a friend who sticks closer than a brother (see Proverbs 18:24). Those who do not know Him can find Him if they seek Him with all their hearts (see Jeremiah 29:13).

Finish the Race

Recently, I read a story about Lisa (not her real name) who decided to try out for her high school track team. Unlike my daughter, Grace, Lisa's talent did not necessarily rest in her physical ability but rather in her love of competition. Because of her sheer determination to represent her team and school, she was eventually selected as the anchor runner for the girls' 4 x 1500-meter relay team. Since her school offered the only 1500-meter relay team in their league, the team was invited to participate in the sectional finals. Most people familiar with the team knew that they had no chance of winning, but many family and friends decided to make the trip to offer their support anyway. When someone asked Lisa why the team chose to go even though they could not compete with the more talented teams, she flashed a smile and said, "We're not very fast. I'm always the last one to finish, so when I come down the stretch, the people in the stands cheer for me."[2]

On the day of the big race at the sectional finals, Lisa's relay team, sure enough, lagged far behind all the other teams. But as Lisa rounded the last corner of the track, running hard for the finish line, her face lit up with the biggest smile. Even though most of the other runners had already left the track, the crowd leaped to its feet and cheered her on until she crossed the finish line.

Personally, I can relate very well with Lisa's approach, especially when it comes to my spiritual journey. To close the distance with God, you do not have to come in ahead of anybody else. You do not even need to follow the cultural dictum that states, "Coming in second is the first to lose." To close the distance, all you need to do is to run the race and smile as you head toward the finish line, if for no other reason than because you know that your GodFather and everyone else in the Kingdom is cheering you on.

You do not have to run faster or work harder than everybody else, and you do not have to rely on your own strength to finish the race. He is "with you always, even to the end of the age." In fact, even right this moment you are nearer to God than you think.

Personal CHALLENGE

How often do we allow the expectations of others to distract us from drawing nearer to our Creator? The combination of our human striving and overwhelming odds, along with our need to finish first, can hold us back so that we do not even run the race.

Countless people hurry through their daily existence without any awareness that God is there to cheer them on through every twist and turn. In the dark, they play hide-and-seek with God and never realize that God is near and never far.

As you come to the end of this book, your journey to come nearer to God is still just beginning. Yet you should have an abiding sense of peace about it, because you do not have to finish first in this race. Your GodFather is not yelling from the stands of heaven, "C'mon! Run faster! Run faster!!" Nor does He want you to heed to the voices around you who are always urging, "C'mon! Go faster! Be better! Work harder!" (These voices may not yet have found a rest stop with God themselves.)

In reality, you can run the race with a smile on your face, knowing that God will cheer you on to the end. Take the time right now to evaluate yourself through the following questions.

Personal EVALUATION

1. Which is your tendency: to invite Jesus to speed through life with you or to notice Jesus at the rest stop?

2. Have you been told that you are not giving God your best if you fail to give Him 100 percent? If so, how have you navigated through the circumstances of life, which fluctuate greatly?

3. Do you have compassion for other Christians who struggle through the fragile moments of life? If you do, how do you express it?

4. Evaluate your spiritual journey. Do you lean toward playing a game of hide-and-seek with God? Have you developed the awareness that He is near and never far?

5. After reading this book, how have you come nearer to God? Have you closed the distance between you and your Creator?

Personal PRAYER

Heavenly Father, I may be finishing this book, but I am continuing my journey to come nearer to You. May the circumstances of life attract me toward You and not distract me away from You. Help me to identify and ignore the voices around me that overwhelm me with messages about human striving and the need to finish first. Help me to run this spiritual race with a smile on my face, knowing that You are there to cheer me on to the end. In Jesus' name, Amen.

Group CHALLENGE

The expectations that we place upon ourselves and the expectations of others can sometimes distract us from our destiny in God. If we feel like we are committed to giving less than 100 percent to God, we may carry a glaring guilt into every area of life. During the celebratory moments of life, we tend to enjoy the brilliance of the light, but during our frail moments, we grope in the darkness.

Fortunately, God is a God of light even on the darkest day. The psalmist provides this extraordinary disclosure concerning God:

> If I say, "Surely the darkness shall fall on me," even the night shall be light about me; indeed, the darkness shall not hide from You, but the night shines as the day; the darkness and the light are both alike to You.
>
> Psalm 139:11–12

What a revelation! God purposes that we live in the light even when it is dark. When others tend to play a game of hide-and-seek in the dark, we can live with the awareness that God is near and never far.

194

As you come to the end of this book, your journey to come nearer to God is still just beginning. Remember that you can run the race with a smile on your face, knowing that God will cheer you on to the end. Discuss as a group where you see yourself within the framework of this chapter.

1. Share what you have discovered about yourself—whether you tend to invite Jesus to speed through life with you or to notice Jesus at the rest stop.

2. Share whether or not you have ever been told that you are not giving God your best if you fail to give Him 100 percent? If you have, how have you learned to navigate through the circumstances of life, which fluctuate greatly?

3. Do you have compassion for other Christians who struggle through the fragile moments of life? If you do, share with the group how you express it.

4. Share with the group what you have discovered about your spiritual journey, whether you lean toward playing a game of hide-and-seek with God or instead have developed the awareness that He is near and never far.

5. Discuss Psalm 139:11–12 and the concept that God is a God of light even on a dark day.

6. Discuss the implications of the idea that coming near to God is really a two-way street: The initial interruption belongs to Him while the lasting response belongs to us.

7. Share with the group how you have come nearer to God and closed the distance between you and your Creator after reading this book.

Notes

Chapter 2 Find the GodFather

1. Ben Sherlock, "10 Most Memorable Quotes from *The Godfather* Trilogy," *Screenrant*, April 3, 2019, https://screenrant.com/best-quotes-godfather-trilogy.

2. NOAA National Weather Service, "Remembering Joplin Tornado," National Weather Service, May 22, 2012, https://www.weather.gov/news/052212-joplin.

3. C. S. Lewis, *The Problem of Pain* (1944; repr., New York: HarperOne, 2001), chap. 6, Kindle.

4. "Whatever will be will be."

5. "Hurricane Katrina," History, August 9, 2019, https://www.history.com/topics/natural-disasters-and-environment/hurricane-katrina.

6. Sherlock, "10 Most Memorable Quotes from *The Godfather* Trilogy."

7. Lewis, *The Problem of Pain*, chap. 6.

Chapter 3 Follow the Real Rock Star

1. Kenneth Partridge, "The 50 Greatest Festivals of All Time," *Billboard*, July 17, 2017, https://www.billboard.com/articles/news/7857778/the-50-greatest-festival-performances-of-all-time.

2. Alexis Petridis, "Beyoncé at Glastonbury 2011—Review," *The Guardian*, June 26, 2011, https://www.theguardian.com/music/2011/jun/27/beyonce-glastonbury-2011-review.

3. Melvyn Ming, Martha Ming, and Steven R. Mills, *LDR Church Development Resource*, vol. 1 (Puyallup, Wash.: Leadership Development Resources, 2010), 17.

4. Henry T. Blackaby and Claude V. King, *Experiencing God: Knowing and Doing the Will of God* (Nashville: Broadman & Holman Publishers, 2004), 2.

5. "Pavarotti in Berlin (5): 165 (!!!) Curtain Calls at Deutsche Oper," *Odd Pavarotti Blog*, August 19, 2012, https://oddpavarottiblog.wordpress.com/2012/08/19/pavarotti-in-berlin-5.

6. P. Douglas Small, *The New Apostolic Epoch* (Charlotte, N.C.: Alive Publications, 2019), 221.

Chapter 4 Download the God App

1. Steven Winkelman, "Appy Birthday: A Brief History of the App Store's First 10 Years," Digital Trends, July 10, 2018, https://www.digitaltrends.com /news/apple-app-store-turns-10.

2. Ian Blair, "Mobile App Download and Usage Statistics," BuildFire, accessed December 11, 2020, https://buildfire.com/app-statistics.

3. Anthony Evans, *Our God Is Awesome* (Chicago: Moody Press, 1994), 22.

Chapter 5 Mind the Gaptivity

1. Josh Linkner, "Why You Must Always 'Mind the Gap' in Your Personal and Professional Life," *Inc.*, February 9, 2016, https://www.inc.com/josh-linkner /mind-the-gap.html.

2. P. Douglas Small, "The Coronavirus—A Window for Change: Seven Things We Must Consider" (white paper), (Charlotte, N.C.: Project Pray, 2020), 16.

3. John Ortberg, quoted in Alan Fadling, *An Unhurried Life: Following Jesus' Rhythms of Work and Rest* (Downers Grove, Ill.: InterVarsity Press, 2020), 8.

4. Shelja Sen, "Babies Need Attuned Mothers to Form Trusting Bond, Not 'Experts,'" *IndianExpress*, May 4, 2019, https://indianexpress.com/article/parent ing/health-fitness/parenting-tips-babies-need-attuned-mothers-not-experts -5709279.

5. Francis Frangipane, *Holiness, Truth, and the Presence of God* (Lake Mary, Fla.: Charisma House, 2011), 63.

6. P. Douglas Small, "Seven Elements of a Solemn Assembly" (white paper), (Charlotte, N.C.: Project Pray, 2013), 10.

7. Linkner, "Why You Must Always 'Mind the Gap.'"

Chapter 6 Hear from Heaven

1. See Matthew 11:15; 13:9, 43; Mark 4:9, 23; 7:16; Luke 8:8; 14:35.

Chapter 7 Enlist as a First Responder

1. Luigi Cavanna, as told to Francesca Berardi, "Heroes of the Front Lines: The Country Won't Work without Them. 12 Stories of People Putting Their Lives on the Line to Help Others during Coronavirus," *Time*, April 9, 2020, https://time .com/collection/coronavirus-heroes/5816885/frontline-workers-coronavirus.

2. Dennis Canale, as told to Paul Moakley, "Heroes of the Front Lines: The Country Won't Work without Them. 12 Stories of People Putting Their Lives on the Line to Help Others during Coronavirus," *Time*, April 9, 2020, https://time .com/collection/coronavirus-heroes/5816885/frontline-workers-coronavirus.

3. Evans, *Our God Is Awesome*, 315.

4. Ruth Haley Barton, *Strengthening the Soul of Your Leadership*, 2nd ed. (Downers Grove, Ill.: InterVarsity Press, 2018), 79.

5. Ralph Waldo Emerson, "Self Reliance" (1841), second paragraph.

6. Mark Batterson, *Soul Print: Discovering Your Divine Destiny* (Colorado Springs: Multnomah Books, 2011), 13.

7. Rick Warren, *Purpose-Driven Life* (Grand Rapids, Mich.: Zondervan, 2002), 242.

8. Os Guinness, *The Call* (Nashville: Word, 1998), 30.

9. Frederick Buechner, *The Alphabet of Grace* (San Francisco: HarperOne, 1989), 14.

Chapter 8 Reproduction over the Production

1. Small, "The New Apostolic Epoch," 251.
2. Small, "The New Apostolic Epoch," 251.
3. George G. Hunter III, "The Church in Post Christian Culture," *Discernment*, 2005, 10 (1, 2), 2.
4. Jay Hemmings, "Remember the Alamo! The Truths and Myths Surrounding the Battle," War History Online, April 13, 2109, https://www.warhistory online.com/instant-articles/truths-and-myths-battle-of-alamo.html.
5. Hemmings, "Remember the Alamo!"
6. Ed Stetzer, "3 Shifts to Increase Outreach," *Outreach*, April 14, 2020, https://outreachmagazine.com/features/evangelism/52152-3-shifts-to-increase -outreach.html.
7. Philip Yancey and Dr. Paul Brand, *In the Likeness of God* (Grand Rapids, Mich.: Zondervan, 2004), 401.
8. Yancey and Brand, *In the Likeness of God*, 401.
9. Yancey and Brand, *In the Likeness of God*, 400.
10. Yancey and Brand, *In the Likeness of God*, 435.
11. Yancey and Brand, *In the Likeness of God*, 437.
12. Earl Creps, *Off-Road Disciplines: Spiritual Adventures of Missional Leaders* (San Francisco: Jossey-Bass, 2006), 117.
13. P. Douglas Small, *The Corona Virus—Is It a Message from God?* (Charlotte, N.C.: Alive Publications, 2020), 9.
14. Nik Ripken, *The Insanity of God: A True Story of Faith Resurrected* (Nashville: B&H Publishing Group, 2013), 302.
15. Ripken, *The Insanity of God*, 310.
16. Ripken, *The Insanity of God*, 311.
17. Stetzer, "3 Shifts to Increase Outreach."
18. Creps, *Off-Road Disciplines*, 117.

Chapter 9 Reflect Your Inner Jesus

1. Benjamin Fearnow, "Elizabeth Warren Celebrates Taking 100,000 'Selfies' with Supporters during 2020 Campaign," *Newsweek*, January 5, 2020, https://www .newsweek.com/elizabeth-warren-celebrates-taking-100000-selfies-supporters -during-2020-campaign-1480473.
2. C. T. Studd, "Only One Life, 'Twill Soon Be Past."

Chapter 10 Cheering You on to the End

1. Mike Yaconelli, *Messy Spirituality* (Grand Rapids, Mich.: Zondervan, 2002), 97.
2. Yaconelli, *Messy Spirituality*, 113.

Dr. Wayman Ming Jr. currently serves as the presiding bishop of the Pentecostal Church of God, which has congregations and members in nearly seventy nations. He is also the founder and president of Exceed International, a church leadership coaching organization. He earned his Doctor of Ministry from the Assemblies of God Theological Seminary and lives in Texas (Dallas–Fort Worth metroplex).

As a follower of Christ, Dr. Wayman Ming Jr. has traveled to over 45 nations, seeking to inspire spiritual reformation for Kingdom advancement. With a passionate plea for "One Mission, One Movement," Dr. Ming believes that maintaining the global mission of the Church remains a biblical mandate for the body of Christ. He also believes that personal reformation is possible for those who intentionally pursue God, and this is the theme of his 2011 book, *Re-Forming a New You: A Guide for Re-Forming Your Heart, Home and Hope.*

Wayman enjoys sipping a hot cup of French vanilla coffee in the mornings and spending time with his wife, Kimberly, their three children and grandson. Their two sons, Spencer and Garrett, are married. They serve at the International Mission Center for the Pentecostal Church of God. Their daughter, Grace, is planning for college. For more information about Dr. Ming, go to his websites waymanming.com or exceedinternational.com. Or visit him on social media: Instagram (@waymanming), Twitter (@waymanming) or Facebook (@waymanmingjr).